乒乓球竞赛规则
（2022）

中国乒乓球协会　审定

北京体育大学出版社

策划编辑：李志诚　潘　帅
责任编辑：李志诚　仝杨杨
责任校对：原子茜
版式设计：华泰联合

图书在版编目 (CIP) 数据

乒乓球竞赛规则 . 2022 / 中国乒乓球协会审定 . --
北京：北京体育大学出版社 , 2022.10（2024.1 重印）
　　ISBN 978-7-5644-3747-3

　　Ⅰ . ①乒… Ⅱ . ①中… Ⅲ . ①乒乓球运动－竞赛规则
－ 2012 Ⅳ . ① G846.4

中国版本图书馆 CIP 数据核字 (2022) 第 196439 号

乒乓球竞赛规则（2022）　PINGPANGQIU JINGSAI GUIZE（2022）　中国乒乓球协会 审定

出版发行：北京体育大学出版社
地　　址：北京市海淀区农大南路 1 号院 2 号楼 2 层办公 B-212
邮　　编：100084
网　　址：http://cbs.bsu.edu.cn
发 行 部：010-62989320
邮 购 部：北京体育大学出版社读者服务部 010-62989432
印　　刷：三河市龙大印装有限公司
开　　本：880 mm×1230 mm　　1/32
成品尺寸：145 mm×210 mm
印　　张：6.125
字　　数：142 千字
版　　次：2022 年 10 月第 1 版
印　　次：2024 年 1 月第 4 次印刷
定　　价：35.00 元

出版说明

《乒乓球竞赛规则（2016）》中文版出版后，国际乒乓球联合会对若干条款进行了修订（以蓝底文字表示）。现根据英文新版《2022年国际乒乓球联合会手册》编译出版《乒乓球竞赛规则（2022）》中文版。

本次编译的内容：乒乓球比赛规则；国际竞赛规程；世界级比赛、奥运会比赛及残疾人奥运会比赛规程。

为使我国裁判员、运动员、教练员、竞赛官员，以及广大乒乓球爱好者更好地学习、掌握和运用规则，本次仍采用中英文对照形式出版。本规则既适用于国际比赛，也适用于国内比赛。

参加本次规则编译、校对、审核的人员：冯政、徐昱玫、张瑛秋、吴飞、赖勇辉、彭华、王欣、孙麒麟、张桦、代天云、赵霞等。

中国乒乓球协会
2022年9月

目 录
CONTENTS

第一章 章 程（略）

第二章　乒乓球比赛规则

2.1　球台

2.1.1　球台的上层表面叫作比赛台面，应为水平放置的长方形，长 2.74 米，宽 1.525 米，离地面高 76 厘米。

2.1.2　比赛台面不包括球台台面的垂直侧面。

2.1.3　比赛台面可用任何材料制成，应具有一致的弹性，即当标准球从离台面 30 厘米高处落至台面时，弹起高度应约为 23 厘米。

2.1.4　比赛台面应呈均匀的暗色，无光泽。沿每个 2.74 米的比赛台面边缘各有一条 2 厘米宽的白色边线，沿每个 1.525 米的比赛台面边缘各有一条 2 厘米宽的白色端线。

2.1.5　比赛台面由一个与端线平行的垂直球网划分为 2 个相等的台区，各台区的整个面积应是一个整体。

2.1.6　双打时，各台区应由一条 3 毫米宽的白色中线划分为 2 个相等的"半区"。中线与边线平行，该中线应视为右半区的一部分。

2.2　球网装置

2.2.1　球网装置包括球网、悬网绳、网柱及将它们固定在球台上的夹钳部分。

2.2.2　球网应悬挂在一根绳子上，绳子两端系在高 15.25 厘米的垂直网柱上，网柱外缘离开边线外缘的距离为

15.25 厘米。

2.2.3　　整个球网的顶端应距离比赛台面 15.25 厘米。

2.2.4　　整个球网的底边应尽量紧贴比赛台面，其两端应整体
与网柱完全相连。

2.3　　球

2.3.1　　球应为圆球体，直径为 40 毫米。

2.3.2　　球重 2.7 克。

2.3.3　　球应用赛璐珞或类似的塑料制成，呈白色或橙色，且
无光泽。

2.4　　球拍

2.4.1　　球拍的大小、形状和重量不限，但底板应平整、坚硬。

2.4.2　　底板中天然木材的厚度至少应占其总厚度的 85%；底
板内部的黏合层可以用碳纤维、玻璃纤维或压缩纸等
纤维材料加固，每层黏合层的厚度不超过底板总厚度
的 7.5% 或 0.35 毫米，两者取其小。

2.4.3　　用来击球的拍面应用一层颗粒向外的普通颗粒胶覆
盖，连同黏合剂，厚度不超过 2 毫米；或用颗粒向内
或向外的海绵胶覆盖，连同黏合剂，厚度不超过 4 毫米。

2.4.3.1　　普通颗粒胶是单层无泡沫的天然橡胶或合成橡胶，其
颗粒必须以每平方厘米不少于 10 颗、不多于 30 颗的
密度平均分布整个表面。

2.4.3.2　　海绵胶是在一层泡沫橡胶上覆盖一层普通颗粒胶，普
通颗粒胶的厚度不超过 2 毫米。

2.4.4　　底板、底板中的任何夹层以及用来击球一面的任何覆

盖物及黏合层均应为厚度均匀的一个整体。可以添加用于制作执握球拍手柄的材料。

2.4.5 覆盖物应覆盖整个拍面，但不得超过其边缘。靠近拍柄部分以及手指执握部分可不予以覆盖，也可用任何材料覆盖。

2.4.6 球拍两面不论是否有覆盖物均应无光泽，一面为黑色，另一面为与黑色及比赛用球颜色有明显区别的鲜艳颜色。

2.4.7 球拍覆盖物不得经过任何物理的、化学的或其他处理。

2.4.7.1 拍面的整体性和颜色上的一致性出现轻微差异，或者加上辅助性或保护性配件，只要未明显改变拍面的性能，可以允许使用。

2.4.8 比赛开始前及比赛过程中运动员需要更换球拍时，应向对方和裁判员展示他（她）将要使用的球拍，并允许他们检查。

2.5 定义

2.5.1 回合：球处于比赛状态的一段时间。

2.5.2 球处于比赛状态：从发球时球被有意抛出前静止在不执拍手掌上的最后一瞬间开始，直到该回合被判重发球或得分。

2.5.3 重发球：不予判分的回合。

2.5.4 一分：判一方得分的回合。

2.5.5 执拍手：正握着球拍的手。

2.5.6 不执拍手：未握着球拍的手；不执拍手臂：不执拍手的手臂。

2.5.7 击球：用握在手中的球拍或执拍手手腕以下部分触及

处于比赛状态的球。

2.5.8 阻挡：当球处于比赛状态时，对方击球后，在比赛台面上方或向比赛台面方向运动的球，尚未触及本方台区，即触及本方运动员或其穿戴（带）的任何物品。

2.5.9 发球员：在一个回合中首先击球的运动员。

2.5.10 接发球员：在一个回合中第二个击球的运动员。

2.5.11 裁判员：被指定管理一场比赛的人。

2.5.12 副裁判员：被指定协助裁判员在某些方面做出判决的人。

2.5.13 运动员穿戴（带）的任何物品，包括他（她）在一个回合开始时穿戴（带）的任何物品，但不包括比赛用球。

2.5.14 球台的端线，包括端线两端的无限延长线。

2.6 发球

2.6.1 发球开始时，球自然地置于不持拍手的手掌上，手掌张开，保持静止。

2.6.2 随后发球员须将球几乎垂直地向上抛起，不得使球旋转，并使球在离开不执拍手的手掌之后上升不少于 16 厘米，球在上升和下降至击球前不应触及任何物品。

2.6.3 当球从抛起的最高点下降时，发球员方可击球，使球首先触及本方台区，然后直接触及接发球员台区。在双打中，球应先后触及发球员和接发球员的右半区。

2.6.4 从发球开始，到球被击出，球要始终在比赛台面的水平面以上和发球员的端线以外；而且从接发球方看，球不能被发球员或其双打同伴的身体或他（她）们所穿戴（带）的任何物品挡住。

2.6.5　　　　球一旦被抛起，发球员的不执拍手及其手臂应立即从球和球网之间的空间移开。

球和球网之间的空间由球和球网及其向上的无限延伸来界定。

2.6.6　　　　运动员发球时，有责任让裁判员或副裁判员确信他（她）的发球符合规则的要求，且裁判员或副裁判员均可判定发球不合法。

2.6.6.1　　　如果裁判员或副裁判员对发球的合法性不确定，在一场比赛中第一次出现时，可以中断比赛并警告发球方。但此后如该运动员或其双打同伴的发球不是明显合法的，将被判发球违例。

2.6.7　　　　运动员因身体残疾而不能遵守合法发球的某些规定时，可由裁判员酌情放宽执行有关规定。

2.7　　　　还击

2.7.1　　　　对方发球或还击后，本方运动员应击球，使球直接触及对方台区，或触及球网装置后，再触及对方台区。

2.8　　　　比赛中的击球次序

2.8.1　　　　在单打中，首先由发球员发球，再由接发球员还击，然后发球员和接发球员交替还击。

2.8.2　　　　在双打中，除2.8.3条款的情况之外，首先由发球员发球，再由接发球员还击，然后由发球员的同伴还击，再由接发球员的同伴还击。此后，运动员按此次序轮流还击。

2.8.3　　　　在双打中，当配对中至少有一名运动员由于身体残疾而坐轮椅时，首先由发球员发球，接发球员应还击，此后该配对的任何一名运动员均可还击。

2.9　重发球

2.9.1　回合出现下列情况应判重发球：

2.9.1.1　如果发球员发出的球触及球网装置后成为合法发球或被接发球员或其同伴阻挡；

2.9.1.2　如果接发球员或其双打同伴未准备好时，球已发出，而且接发球员或其双打同伴没有试图击球；

2.9.1.3　由于发生了运动员无法控制的干扰，而使运动员出现未能合法发球、还击等不能遵守规则的情况；

2.9.1.4　裁判员或副裁判员暂停比赛；

2.9.1.5　由于身体残疾而坐轮椅的运动员在接发球时，发球员进行合法发球之后，出现下列情况：

2.9.1.5.1　球在触及接发球员的台区后，朝着球网方向运行；

2.9.1.5.2　球停在接发球员的台区上；

2.9.1.5.3　在单打中，球在触及接发球员的台区后，从其任意一条边线离开球台。

2.9.2　可以在下列情况下暂停比赛：

2.9.2.1　由于要纠正发球、接发球次序或方位错误；

2.9.2.2　由于要实行轮换发球法；

2.9.2.3　由于警告、处罚运动员或指导者；

2.9.2.4　由于比赛环境受到干扰，以致该回合结果有可能受到影响。

2.10　一分

2.10.1　除判重发球外，一个回合出现下列情况该运动员得1分：

2.10.1.1　对方运动员未能合法发球；

2.10.1.2　对方运动员未能合法还击；

2.10.1.3　运动员在发球或还击后，对方运动员在击球前，球触及了除球网装置以外的任何东西；

2.10.1.4　对方击球后，球没有触及本方台区而越过本方台区或端线；

2.10.1.5　对方击球后，球穿过球网，或从球网和网柱之间、球网和比赛台面之间通过；

2.10.1.6　对方阻挡；

2.10.1.7　对方故意连续2次击球；

2.10.1.8　对方用不符合2.4.3、2.4.4和2.4.5条款的拍面击球；

2.10.1.9　对方运动员或其穿戴（带）的任何东西使比赛台面移动；

2.10.1.10　对方运动员或其穿戴（带）的任何东西触及球网装置；

2.10.1.11　对方运动员不执拍手触及比赛台面；

2.10.1.12　双打时，对方运动员击球次序错误；

2.10.1.13　执行轮换发球法时，出现2.15.4条款情况。

2.10.1.14　如果双方运动员或双打配对由于身体残疾而坐轮椅：

2.10.1.14.1　对方击球时，其大腿后部未能和轮椅或坐垫保持最低限度的接触；

2.10.1.14.2　对方击球前，其任意一只手触及比赛球台；

2.10.1.14.3　在比赛状态中对方的脚垫或脚触及地面。

2.10.1.15　当对方双打配对至少有一名为轮椅运动员时，其轮椅的任何部分或其站立运动员脚部的任何部分超越球台中线的假定延长线。

2.11   一局比赛

2.11.1   在一局比赛中，先得 11 分的一方为胜方；当双方均得到 10 分后，先领先对方 2 分的一方为胜方。

2.12   一场比赛

2.12.1   一场比赛由奇数局组成。

2.13   发球、接发球次序和方位

2.13.1   选择首先发球、接发球和方位的权力应由抽签来决定。中签者可以选择先发球或先接发球，或选择在某一方位开始比赛。

2.13.2   当一方运动员选择了先发球或先接发球，或者选择了在某一方位开始比赛，另一方运动员应做出另一个选择。

2.13.3   在每 2 分之后，接发球方即成为发球方，依此类推，直至该局比赛结束，或者直至双方比分都达到 10 分或实行轮换发球法，这时，发球和接发球次序仍然不变，但每人只轮发 1 分球。

2.13.4   双打的第一局比赛，先由有发球权的一方确定第一发球员，再由接发球方确定第一接发球员；以后的每局比赛，由先发球的一方确定第一发球员，第一接发球员则是前一局发球给他（她）的运动员。

2.13.5   在双打中，每次换发球时，前面的接发球员应成为发球员，前面的发球员的同伴应成为接发球员。

2.13.6　一局中首先发球的一方，在该场下一局应首先接发球。在双打决胜局中，当一方先得 5 分时，接发球方应交换接发球次序。

2.13.7　一局中，在某一方位比赛的一方，在该场下一局应换到另一方位。在决胜局中，一方先得 5 分时，双方应交换方位。

2.14　发球、接发球次序和方位的错误

2.14.1　裁判员一旦发现发球、接发球次序错误，应立即暂停比赛，并按该场比赛开始时确立的次序，按场上比分由应该发球或接发球的运动员发球或接发球；在双打中，则按发现错误时那一局中首先有发球权的一方所确立的次序进行纠正，继续比赛。

2.14.2　裁判员一旦发现运动员应交换方位而未交换时，应立即暂停比赛，并按该场比赛开始时确立的次序，按场上比分运动员的正确方位进行纠正，继续比赛。

2.14.3　在任何情况下，发现错误之前的所有得分均有效。

2.15　轮换发球法

2.15.1　除 2.15.2 条款的情况之外，一局比赛进行到 10 分钟或双方运动员有此请求时，应实行轮换发球法。

2.15.2　如果一局比赛比分达到 18 分，将不实行轮换发球法。

2.15.3　当时限到且须实行轮换发球法时，球处于比赛状态，裁判员应立即暂停比赛，由被暂停回合的发球员发球，继续比赛；如果实行轮换发球法时，球未处于比赛状态，应由前一回合的接发球员发球，继续比赛。

2.15.4　此后，每位运动员应轮发 1 分球，直到该局结束。如果接发球方进行了 13 次合法还击，则判接发球方得 1 分。

2.15.5　实行轮换发球法不能更改该场比赛中按 2.13.6 条款所确定的发球与接发球次序。

2.15.6　轮换发球法一经实行，将一直执行到该场比赛结束。

第三章 国际竞赛规程

3.1 规则和规程的适用范围

3.1.1 比赛类型

3.1.1.1 国际竞赛，即一个以上协会的运动员参加的比赛。

3.1.1.2 国际比赛，即不同协会代表队之间的一场比赛。

3.1.1.3 公开赛，即所有协会的运动员均可报名参加的比赛。

3.1.1.4 限制赛，即除年龄组外只限于特定组别的运动员参加的比赛。

3.1.1.5 邀请赛，即限于个别邀请的、指定协会或运动员参加的比赛。

3.1.2 适用范围

3.1.2.1 除 3.1.2.2 条款及参赛协会达成另外协议的国际比赛之外，规则（即第二章）适用于冠以世界、洲、奥林匹克和残疾人奥林匹克名称的比赛，以及公开赛和国际比赛。

3.1.2.2 国际乒联执行委员会可授权公开赛的组织者采用临时变更的规则。

3.1.2.3 国际竞赛规程应适用于下列比赛：

3.1.2.3.1 冠以世界、奥林匹克和残疾人奥林匹克名称的比赛，除非理事会许可了另外的规程，并事先通知了各参赛协会；

3.1.2.3.2 洲的比赛，除非有关洲联合会许可了另外的规程，并事先通知了各参赛协会；

3.1.2.3.3　国际公开锦标赛（3.7.1.2），除非国际乒联执行委员会许可了另外的规程，并根据 3.1.2.4 条款事先通知了各参赛协会；

3.1.2.3.4　公开赛，3.1.2.4 条款规定的除外。

3.1.2.4　不依照本规程任何条款而举办的公开赛，应在报名表中说明变更内容的性质和范围；填写并提交报名表应被视为报名者同意包括变更内容在内的比赛条件。

3.1.2.5　建议本规则和规程适用于所有国际比赛；但在遵守章程的条件下，非会员单位组织的国际限制赛、邀请赛以及经许可的国际比赛，可以按照主办机构制定的规则举行。

3.1.2.6　本规则和国际竞赛规程被认为适用于所有国际比赛，除非变更内容已事先得到同意，或明确写入已公布的竞赛规则中。

3.1.2.7　对规则的详细解释和说明，包括国际竞赛的器材规格，应由理事会公布为《技术或管理文件》；操作指引或实施程序可由执行委员会颁布为《手册》或《指南》。此类出版物既包括强制性部分也包括建议或指导。

3.2　器材和比赛条件

3.2.1　批准和许可的器材

3.2.1.1　对比赛器材的批准和许可，应由器材委员会代表理事会执行；执行委员会可随时中止某一项批准或许可，随后理事会可撤销该项批准或许可。

3.2.1.2　公开赛的报名表或竞赛指南应详细说明将使用的球

台、球网装置、地胶及球的品牌和颜色；应由国际乒联或比赛所在地的协会从国际乒联现行批准的品牌和型号中挑选并确定球台、球网装置及球。对于指定的国际乒联批准赛事，地胶应是国际乒联现行批准的品牌和型号。

3.2.1.3 覆盖球拍的任何普通颗粒胶或海绵胶应是国际乒联现行许可的，且国际乒联标志、国际乒联编号（如有）、供应商名称和商标名应在最靠近拍柄处清晰可见。

国际乒联办公室负责更新所有批准和授权的器材和材料清单，详细资料可从国际乒联网站上获得。

3.2.1.4 轮椅运动员比赛使用的球台，其桌腿距离球台端线至少要 40 厘米。

3.2.2 比赛服装

3.2.2.1 比赛服装包括短袖或无袖运动衫和短裤或短裙；或连体运动服（裙）；短袜和运动鞋；其他服装，如半套或全套运动服，未经裁判长允许不得在比赛时穿着。

3.2.2.2 短袖运动衫（袖子和领子除外）、短裤或短裙的主要颜色应与比赛用球的颜色明显不同。

3.2.2.3 在运动员短袖运动衫的后背可印有号码或文字，用于标明运动员、运动员的协会，或在俱乐部比赛时，标明运动员的俱乐部，以及符合 3.2.5.9 条款所规定的广告。如果短袖运动衫的背后印有运动员的姓名，应该在紧靠衣领下方的位置。

3.2.2.4 在短袖运动衫背部的中间位置应优先佩戴主办方指定的用于标明运动员身份的号码布，而不是广告。这个号码布应是长方形，面积不超过 600 平方厘米。

3.2.2.5　在比赛服装前面或侧面的任何标记或装饰物，以及运动员佩戴的任何物品，如珠宝装饰等，均不应过于显眼或反光，以免影响对方的视线。

3.2.2.6　服装上不得带有可能产生不悦或诋毁本项运动声誉的设计和字样。

3.2.2.7　在冠以世界、奥林匹克或残疾人奥林匹克名称的比赛中，团体赛同队运动员，以及来自同一协会的双打配对，应穿着相同的服装，鞋、袜及服装上广告的数量、尺寸、颜色和设计可以不同。

3.2.2.8　比赛的双方运动员应穿着颜色明显不同的运动衫，以使观众能够容易地区分他们。

3.2.2.9　当双方运动员或运动队所穿短袖运动衫类似且就哪一方更换无法达成一致意见时，应由裁判员通过抽签做出决定。

3.2.2.10　运动员参加冠以世界、奥林匹克或残疾人奥林匹克名称的比赛，穿着的短袖运动衫、短裤或短裙等应为其协会批准的种类。

3.2.3　比赛条件

3.2.3.1　比赛空间应为不小于14米长、7米宽、5米高的长方体，但4个角可用长度不超过1.5米的挡板围蔽。轮椅项目的比赛空间可以减小，但不得小于8米长、6米宽。元老赛事的比赛空间可以减小，但不得小于10米长、5米宽。

3.2.3.2　以下器材和装置应被视为每个比赛区域的一部分：球台及球网装置，球台号，地胶，裁判员桌椅，比分显示器，毛巾盒和球盒，挡板，挡板上显示运动员姓名或协会名称的标志牌，且应安放妥当、不影响比赛的小型技术器材。

3.2.3.3　比赛区域应由挡板围蔽，以便与相邻的比赛区域及观众隔开，挡板高 75 厘米，底色为同一深色。

3.2.3.4　在冠以世界、奥林匹克和残疾人奥林匹克名称的比赛中，从比赛台面高度测得的照明度不得低于 1500 勒克斯，且整个比赛台面照明度均匀，比赛区域其他地方的照明度不得低于 1000 勒克斯；其他比赛中，比赛台面的照明度不得低于 1000 勒克斯且照明度均匀，比赛区域其他地方的照明度不得低于 600 勒克斯。

3.2.3.5　使用多张球台时，每张球台的照明水平应是一致的，比赛场馆的背景照明不得高于比赛区域的最低照明度。

3.2.3.6　光源距离地面不得少于 5 米。

3.2.3.7　场地四周一般应为暗色，不应有明亮光源，或从未加遮盖的窗户或缝隙等透过的日光。

3.2.3.8　地板不应为浅色、反光强烈或打滑，而且应当具有弹性；轮椅比赛的地板可以是坚硬的。

3.2.3.8.1　在冠以世界、奥林匹克和残疾人奥林匹克名称的比赛中，地板应为木质或国际乒联许可的品牌和种类的可卷曲合成材料。

3.2.3.9　球网装置上的技术器材应被视为该球网装置的一部分。

3.2.4　球拍检测

3.2.4.1　每个运动员有责任确保用于粘贴球拍覆盖物的黏合剂不含有毒挥发溶剂。

3.2.4.2　在所有冠以世界、奥林匹克和残疾人奥林匹克名称的国际乒联比赛中，以及国际乒联所挑选的部分其他比赛中，应建立球拍检测中心，也可在洲和地区的比赛中建立球拍检测中心。

3.2.4.2.1　球拍检测中心应按照执行委员会根据器材委员会和裁判员与裁判长委员会的建议所制定的政策和程序进行球拍检测，确保球拍在包括但不限于平整度、覆盖物厚度、各层均匀厚度和连续性、是否含有有害挥发性物质等方面符合国际乒联规程的规定。

3.2.4.2.2　球拍检测通常在赛前进行。仅当球拍未按时提交赛前检测，或赛前无法进行检测时才进行赛后检测。

3.2.4.2.3　没有通过赛前检测的球拍不能使用，但可以用第二块球拍替代，如果时间允许立即检测，如果时间不允许将在赛后检测；如果球拍没有通过赛后的抽检，该运动员将受到处罚。

3.2.4.2.4　运动员有权在赛前自愿进行球拍检测，且不受任何处罚。

3.2.4.3　在 4 年内累计 4 次未能通过球拍检测的任意一项，该运动员可以完成该赛事，但随后执行委员会将暂停该运动员参加国际乒联的赛事 12 个月。

3.2.4.3.1　国际乒联将以书面形式通知被停赛的运动员。

3.2.4.3.2　被停赛的运动员可以在收到停赛函的 21 天之内向国际乒联仲裁法庭申诉；即使提交了申诉，对该运动员的停赛仍有效。

3.2.4.4　从 2010 年 9 月 1 日起，国际乒联将对所有的球拍检测不合格情况进行登记。

3.2.4.5　应提供一处通风良好的地方用于粘贴球拍覆盖物，比赛场馆的任何其他地方不得使用液体黏合剂。

"比赛场馆"指建筑物中用于乒乓球及其相关活动的

设施和公共区域部分。

3.2.5 广告和标记物

3.2.5.1 在比赛区域内，广告只能在 3.2.3.2 条款中所列的器材与装置上或比赛服装、裁判员服装、运动员号码布上展示，不应有额外的特别展示。

3.2.5.1.1 比赛区域内及周边、比赛服装、裁判员服装、运动员号码布上的广告和标记物不得含烟草产品、酒精饮料、有害药物和非法产品的内容，也不得含种族、仇外、性别、宗教和残疾方面的歧视内容或暗示，以及其他形式的歧视。然而，对并非明确为 18 岁以下运动员组织的比赛，只要当地法律允许，国际乒联可以允许在比赛区域内或周边的器材或设备上出现含非蒸馏酒精饮料的广告或标志物。

3.2.5.2 在奥运会和残奥会中，比赛器材、比赛服装以及裁判员服装上的广告应分别符合国际奥委会和国际残奥委会章程的规定。

3.2.5.3 比赛区域除两边挡板上的 LED 和类似装置的广告外，整个比赛区域的任何地方不允许有其他荧光、冷光或反光的颜色，挡板的背景颜色应保持暗色调。

3.2.5.3.1 在比赛中，挡板上的广告不允许由暗变亮或由亮变暗。

3.2.5.3.2 在比赛中，挡板上的 LED 和类似装置不能过于明亮以至于影响到运动员，且球处于比赛状态时不允许变换 LED 和类似装置上的广告。

3.2.5.3.3 没有得到国际乒联批准的广告不允许在 LED 和类似装置上使用。

3.2.5.4 挡板内侧的字样和标记应与比赛用球的颜色明显不同，

且不得超过两种颜色，其总高度应限制在 40 厘米之内。

3.2.5.5 　　比赛区域地面最多可有 6 个广告，这些广告：

3.2.5.5.1 　　在球台每端可各有 2 个广告，每个广告的总面积不得超过 5 平方米；在球台每侧可各有 1 个广告，每个广告的总面积不得超过 2.5 平方米；

3.2.5.5.2 　　两端的广告与球台端线的距离不得少于 3 米；

3.2.5.5.3 　　必须颜色一致且与比赛用球的颜色不同，使用其他颜色须事先得到国际乒联的同意；

3.2.5.5.4 　　不得明显改变地板表面的摩擦力；

3.2.5.5.5 　　只能包含一个标识、字标或其他图标，并且不得有任何背景。

3.2.5.6 　　球台上的广告必须符合下列要求：

3.2.5.6.1 　　在球台每个半区的侧面和端面均可以有 1 个制造商或供应商名称或标识的永久性广告。

3.2.5.6.2 　　在球台每个半区的侧面和端面均可以有 1 个临时性广告，临时性广告也可以是制造商或供应商名称或标识。

3.2.5.6.3 　　每个永久性广告和每个临时性广告的总长度不超过 60 厘米。

3.2.5.6.4 　　临时性广告应与永久性广告明显分开。

3.2.5.6.5 　　不能是其他乒乓球器材供应商广告。

3.2.5.6.6 　　在球台底架上不得有广告、球台名称、球台制造商或供应商名称或标识，除非球台制造商或供应商也是赛事的冠名赞助商。

3.2.5.7 　　球网在球台上的每边可有 2 个临时性广告，必须与比赛用球的颜色明显不同，与球网顶端距离不少于 3 厘米；球台边线垂直延伸部分的球网广告应为标志、文字或其他图标。

3.2.5.8　比赛区域内裁判桌或其他器材上的广告，其任何一面的总面积不得超过 750 平方厘米。

3.2.5.9　比赛服装上的广告仅限于：

3.2.5.9.1　制造厂家的常规商标、标志或名称，总面积不得超过 24 平方厘米；

3.2.5.9.2　短袖运动衫的前面、侧面或肩部不得超过 6 条广告，每条广告必须明显分开，广告总面积不得超过 600 平方厘米；而且短袖运动衫正面的广告不得超过 4 条。

3.2.5.9.3　短袖运动衫的背后不得超过 2 条广告，总面积不得超过 400 平方厘米。

3.2.5.9.4　短裤或短裙上不得超过 2 条广告，总面积不得超过 120 平方厘米，且只能出现在正面和侧面。

3.2.5.10　运动员号码布上的广告总面积不得超过 100 平方厘米。如果不使用号码布，可以为赛事赞助商提供总面积不超过 100 平方厘米的额外临时广告。

3.2.5.11　裁判员服装上的广告总面积不得超过 40 平方厘米。

3.2.6　兴奋剂检测

3.2.6.1　所有参加国际竞赛，包括青少年比赛的运动员均应接受赛时由国际乒联、运动员所属协会和其他任何在该项比赛中负责检测的反兴奋剂机构所进行的兴奋剂检测。

3.2.7　乒乓球回放系统

3.2.7.1　当运动员对负责本场比赛的裁判员就事实做出的决定提出申诉时，可使用乒乓球回放系统（TTR）。TTR 将回放导致某一判决的情况，并由 TTR 官员做出最终决定。

3.3　　　比赛官员

3.3.1　　裁判长

3.3.1.1　　每次竞赛应指派一名裁判长，其身份和工作地点应告知所有参赛者，并适时告知各参赛队队长。

3.3.1.2　　裁判长应对下列事项负责：

3.3.1.2.1　主持抽签；

3.3.1.2.2　编排比赛日程（时间、台号）；

3.3.1.2.3　指派裁判员；

3.3.1.2.4　主持裁判员的赛前短会；

3.3.1.2.5　审查运动员的参赛资格；

3.3.1.2.6　决定在紧急时刻能否中断比赛；

3.3.1.2.7　决定在一场比赛中运动员能否离开比赛区域；

3.3.1.2.8　决定能否延长法定练习时间；

3.3.1.2.9　决定在一场比赛中运动员能否穿长运动服；

3.3.1.2.10　对解释规则和规程的任何问题做出决定，包括服装、比赛器材和比赛条件的可接受性；

3.3.1.2.11　决定在比赛紧急中断时，运动员能否练习，以及练习地点；

3.3.1.2.12　对于不良行为或其他违反规程的行为采取纪律行动。

3.3.1.3　　经竞赛管理委员会的同意，当裁判长的任何职责托付给其他人员时，这些人员中的每个人的具体职责和工作地点应告知参赛者，并适时告知各参赛队队长。

3.3.1.4　　裁判长或在其缺席时负责代理的副裁判长，在比赛过程中自始至终应亲临比赛场地。

3.3.1.5　　如果裁判长认为必要，可在任何时间更换裁判人员，但不得更改被更换者在其职权范围内就事实问题做出的判定。

3.3.1.6　从抵达比赛场馆开始直至离开场馆，运动员应处于裁判长的管辖之下。

3.3.2　裁判员、副裁判员、计数员和乒乓球回放系统官员

3.3.2.1　每场比赛均应指派 1 名裁判员和 1 名副裁判员。

3.3.2.2　裁判员应坐或站在球台一侧，与球网成一直线。副裁判员应面对裁判员坐在球台另一侧。

3.3.2.3　裁判员应对下列事项负责：

3.3.2.3.1　检查比赛器材和比赛条件的可接受性，如有问题向裁判长报告；

3.3.2.3.2　按 3.4.2.1.1 和 3.4.2.1.2 条款规定，任意取一个球；

3.3.2.3.3　主持抽签确定发球、接发球次序和方位；

3.3.2.3.4　决定是否由于运动员身体伤残而放宽合法发球的某些规定；

3.3.2.3.5　控制方位和发球、接发球的次序，纠正出现的错误；

3.3.2.3.6　决定每一个回合得 1 分或重发球；

3.3.2.3.7　根据规定的程序报分；

3.3.2.3.8　在适当的时间执行轮换发球法；

3.3.2.3.9　保持比赛的连续性；

3.3.2.3.10　对违反场外指导或行为等规定者采取行动；

3.3.2.3.11　如果双方运动员或运动队所穿短袖运动衫类似且双方就哪一方更换无法达成一致意见时，抽签决定某一方必须更换；

3.3.2.3.12　确保只有经许可的人员才能进入比赛区域。

3.3.2.4　副裁判员应：

3.3.2.4.1　决定处于比赛状态中的球是否触及球台距离他（她）

最近一侧比赛台面的上边缘；

3.3.2.4.2　　有违反场外指导或行为规定情况时，告知裁判员。

3.3.2.5　　　裁判员或副裁判员均可：

3.3.2.5.1　　判决运动员发球动作不合法；

3.3.2.5.2　　判决合法发球触及球网装置；

3.3.2.5.3　　判决运动员阻挡；

3.3.2.5.4　　判决比赛条件受到意外干扰，该回合的结果有可能受到影响；

3.3.2.5.5　　对练习时间、比赛时间及间歇时间进行计时。

3.3.2.6　　　执行轮换发球法时，副裁判员或另外指派的一名裁判人员均可担任计数员，数接发球方运动员的击球板数。

3.3.2.7　　　裁判员不得否决副裁判员根据3.3.2.5条款所做的决定。

3.3.2.8　　　当启用乒乓球回放系统（TTR）时，裁判员或副裁判员做出的决定可能会被 TTR 官员否决。

3.3.2.9　　　从抵达比赛区域开始直至离开，运动员应处于裁判员的管辖之下。

3.3.3　申诉

3.3.3.1　　　在单项比赛中的双方运动员或在团体比赛中的双方队长之间所达成的协议，均不能改变负责该场比赛的裁判人员就事实问题所做的决定，亦不能改变裁判长就解释规则或规程的问题所做的决定；亦不能改变竞赛管理委员会对竞赛或比赛管理问题所做的决定。

3.3.3.2　　　对有关裁判人员就事实问题所做的决定，不得向裁判长提出申诉；对裁判长就解释规则或规程的问题所做的决定，不得向管理委员会提出申诉。

3.3.3.3　　　当启用乒乓球回放系统（TTR）时，可对负责该场比赛的裁判员就事实做出的决定向 TTR 官员提出申诉，TTR 官员的决定为最终裁决。

3.3.3.4　对裁判人员就解释规则或规程的问题所做的决定不服时，可以向裁判长提出申诉，裁判长的决定为最后决定。

3.3.3.5　对裁判长就未包括在规则或规程中的有关比赛管理问题所做的决定不服时，可向竞赛管理委员会提出申诉，该委员会做出的决定为最后决定。

3.3.3.6　在单项比赛中，只能由参赛的运动员就该场比赛中出现的问题提出申诉；在团体比赛中，则只能由参赛队的队长就比赛中出现的问题提出申诉。

3.3.3.7　对裁判长就解释规则或规程的问题所做的决定或竞赛管理委员会就比赛管理方面的问题所做的决定仍有异议时，可以由有权申诉的运动员或队长通过所属协会将问题提交国际乒联规则委员会考虑。

3.3.3.8　规则委员会将就此做出裁决，作为将来决定的指南。协会仍可就该裁决向理事会或代表大会提出反对，但不影响裁判长或竞赛管理委员会已做出的任何最后决定。

3.4　比赛的管理

3.4.1　报分

3.4.1.1　当回合结束球脱离比赛状态，或在情况允许时，裁判员应立即报分。

3.4.1.1.1　一局比赛中的报分，裁判员应首先报下一回合即将发球一方的得分，然后报对方的得分。

3.4.1.1.2　在一局比赛开始和交换发球权时，裁判员的手势应指向下一发球方，也可以在报完比分后，报出下一回合发球员的姓名。

3.4.1.1.3　一局比赛结束时，裁判员应先报胜方分数，然后报负方分数，然后可以报胜方运动员或配对的姓名。

3.4.1.2　除报分外，裁判员还可以用手势表示他（她）的判决。

3.4.1.2.1　当判得分时，裁判员可将靠近得分方的手臂举起，使上臂水平，前臂垂直，手握拳向上。

3.4.1.2.2　当出于某种原因，回合应被判为重发球时，裁判员可以将手高举过头表示该回合结束。

3.4.1.3　报分，以及在实行轮换发球法时报击球数，裁判员应使用英语或双方运动员及裁判员均能接受的任何其他语言。

3.4.1.4　应使用机械或电子设备显示比分，使运动员和观众都能看清楚。

3.4.1.5　当运动员因不良行为受到正式警告后，应在比分显示器上或比分显示器旁放置一张黄牌。

3.4.2　器材

3.4.2.1　运动员不得在比赛区域内挑球。

3.4.2.1.1　如有可能，在进入比赛区域前，运动员应有机会挑选一个或几个比赛用球，并使用运动员所挑选的球进行比赛。

3.4.2.1.2   如果运动员在进入比赛区域前未挑选比赛用球，或运动员就比赛用球意见不一致，则由裁判员从一盒赛会指定的比赛用球中任意取一个球进行比赛。

3.4.2.1.3   如果比赛中球损坏，应由赛前选定的另外一个球替换；如果没有赛前选定的球，则由裁判员从一盒赛会指定的比赛用球中任意取一个球替换。

3.4.2.2   应使用经过国际乒联许可的球拍覆盖物，且不得用任何物理、化学或其他方式进行处理而改变其击球性能、摩擦力、外观、颜色、结构、表面等；特别是不得使用添加剂。

3.4.2.3   球拍必须能顺利通过球拍检测的各项参数。

3.4.2.4   在一场单项比赛中，不允许更换球拍，除非球拍意外严重损坏到不能使用。如果球拍发生意外损坏，运动员应立即替换随身带至比赛区域的另外一块球拍，或递入比赛区域的球拍。

3.4.2.5   运动员在比赛间歇时，应将球拍留在比赛球台上，得到裁判员的另外许可时除外；但如果球拍捆绑在运动员手上，裁判员应允许运动员在比赛间歇不摘下球拍。

3.4.3   练习

3.4.3.1   在一场比赛即将开始前，运动员有权在比赛球台上练习不超过 2 分钟，正常间歇不能练习；只有裁判长有权将规定的练习时间延长。

3.4.3.2   在紧急中断比赛时，裁判长可允许运动员在任何球台上练习，包括比赛球台。

3.4.3.3   运动员应有合理的机会检查和熟悉将要使用的器材，但这并不意味着运动员在替换损坏的球或球拍后，有权在**恢复**比赛前练习超过几个来回。

3.4.4　间歇

3.4.4.1　一场单项比赛应连续进行，但任何一方运动员均有以下权利：

3.4.4.1.1　在单项比赛的局与局之间，有不超过 1 分钟的间歇；

3.4.4.1.2　单项比赛的每局开始后，每 6 分后或决胜局交换方位时，可用短暂的时间擦汗。

3.4.4.2　一名运动员（单打）或一对运动员（双打）可在一场单项比赛中要求一次暂停，时间不超过 1 分钟。

3.4.4.2.1　在单项比赛中，暂停应由运动员或指定的场外指导者提出；在团体比赛中，应由运动员或队长提出。

3.4.4.2.2　当一名运动员或一对运动员与其指导者或队长对是否暂停有不同意见时，在单项比赛中决定权属于这名运动员或这对运动员，在团体比赛中决定权属于队长。

3.4.4.2.3　请求暂停只有在一局比赛的回合之间做出，应用双手做出"T"形表示。

3.4.4.2.4　在得到某方合理的暂停请求后，裁判员应暂停比赛，用靠近请求暂停方一侧的手出示白牌；白牌或其他合适的标志物应放置在请求暂停方的台区上。

3.4.4.2.5　当提出暂停的一方运动员准备继续比赛或 1 分钟时间到时（以时间短的为限），白牌或标志物应被拿走并且立即恢复比赛。

3.4.4.2.6　如果比赛双方运动员或其代表同时请求暂停，应在双方运动员准备恢复比赛或 1 分钟时间到时（以时间短的为限）继续比赛。在该场单项比赛中，双方运动员都不再有暂停的权利。

3.4.4.3   一场团体赛中的各场比赛之间没有间歇，除了需要连场的运动员有权在连场比赛的场次之间要求最多5分钟的间歇。

3.4.4.4   运动员因意外事件而暂时丧失比赛能力时，裁判长若认为中断比赛不至于给对方带来不利，可允许中断比赛，但时间要尽量短些，在任何情况下都不得超过10分钟。

3.4.4.5   如果失去比赛能力的状态早已存在，或在比赛开始前就有理由可以预见，或由于比赛的正常紧张状态引起，则不能允许中断比赛。如果失去比赛能力的原因在于运动员当时的身体状况或比赛进行的方式，引起抽筋或过度疲劳，这些也不能成为中断比赛的理由。只有因意外事故，如摔倒受伤而丧失比赛能力，才能允许紧急中断。

3.4.4.6   如果比赛区域内任何人受伤流血，应立即中断比赛，直到伤者接受了治疗且比赛区域内所有血迹都已擦干净后再恢复比赛。

3.4.4.7   除非裁判长允许，运动员在一场单项比赛中应自始至终留在比赛区域内或其附近，在局间间歇和暂停期间，运动员应在裁判员的监督下，留在比赛区域周围3米以内的地方。

3.5   纪律

3.5.1   场外指导

3.5.1.1   团体比赛中，运动员可以接受有权进入比赛区域内的任何人的指导。

3.5.1.2　单项比赛，一名运动员或一对运动员只能接受一个人的场外指导，且应提前向裁判员指定该指导者；如果一对双打运动员来自不同协会，可分别授权一名指导者，但根据 3.5.1 和 3.5.2 条款这 2 位指导者应被视为一体；如未被授权的人进行指导，裁判员应出示红牌令其远离比赛区域。

3.5.1.3　只要没有拖延比赛（3.4.4.1），运动员可以在除比赛回合中的任何时间接受场外指导。如被授权的指导者进行非法指导，裁判员将出示黄牌进行警告，如果再次违反将被驱逐出比赛区域。

3.5.1.4　在同一场团体赛或单项的同一场比赛中，如指导者已被警告过，任何人再进行非法指导，裁判员将出示红牌并将其驱逐出比赛区域，无论其是否曾被警告过。

3.5.1.5　在团体比赛中被驱逐的指导者不允许在团体比赛结束前返回，除非需要他（她）上场比赛，并且也不能被其他指导者代替；在单项比赛中，不允许在该场单项比赛结束前返回。

3.5.1.6　如被驱逐的指导者拒绝离开或在比赛结束前返回，裁判员应中断比赛，立即向裁判长报告。

3.5.1.7　以上规定只限制对比赛的指导，并不限制运动员或队长在需要时就裁判员的决定提出正式申诉，或阻止运动员与翻译或所属协会代表就某项判决的解释进行商议。

3.5.2　不良行为

3.5.2.1　运动员和教练员或其他指导者应该克制可能不公平地影响对手、冒犯观众或影响本项运动声誉的不良行为，诸如辱骂性语言，故意损坏比赛用球或将球击出比赛区域，踢球台或挡板和不尊重比赛官员等。

3.5.2.2　任何时候，运动员和教练员或其他指导者出现严重冒犯行为，裁判员应该中断比赛，立即报告裁判长；如果冒犯行为不太严重，第一次，裁判员可出示黄牌，警告冒犯者，如果再次冒犯将被罚分。

3.5.2.3　除3.5.2.2和3.5.2.5条款规定外，运动员在受到警告后，在同一场单项比赛或团体比赛中第二次冒犯，裁判员应判对方得1分，再犯，判对方得2分，每次罚分应同时出示黄牌和红牌。

3.5.2.4　在同一场单项比赛或团体比赛中，运动员在被判罚3分后继续有不良行为，裁判员应中断比赛并立即报告裁判长。

3.5.2.5　在一场单项比赛中，如果运动员更换了没有损坏的球拍，裁判员应中断比赛，向裁判长报告。

3.5.2.6　双打配对中的任何一名运动员所受到的警告或罚分，应视作是对该配对的，但未冒犯的运动员在同一场团体比赛随后的场次不受影响；双打比赛开始时，双打配对将被视为已经携带2名运动员在同一场团体赛中各自所受到的警告或罚分中的较重处罚。

3.5.2.7　除3.5.2.2条款规定外，如果一名教练员或另一名指导者受到警告后，在同一场单项比赛或团体比赛中再次冒犯，裁判员应出示红牌并将其驱逐出比赛区域，直到该场团体比赛结束或单项赛中的该场单项比赛结束才可返回。

3.5.2.8　无论是否得到裁判员的报告，裁判长都有权取消有严重不公平或冒犯行为运动员的一场、一项或一次赛事的资格；当他（她）采取以上行动时应出示红牌；对于严重程度略轻不足以取消资格的冒犯行为，裁判长可决定向国际乒联纪律小组报告此类行为。

3.5.2.9　如果一名运动员在团体或单项中有 2 场比赛被取消资格，就被自动取消其参加该团体或单项所有比赛的资格。

3.5.2.10　裁判长有权取消已经 2 次被驱逐出比赛区域的任何人参加本次赛事剩余比赛的资格。

3.5.2.11　如果一名运动员因任何原因被取消一项比赛或整个赛事的资格，他（她）将自动丧失任何相关的头衔、奖牌、奖金或排名积分。

3.5.2.12　对于十分严重的不良行为，应向冒犯者所属协会通报。

3.5.2.13　国际乒联纪律小组将对任何严重、屡次、持续违反 3.5.2 条款的行为采取进一步的行动，并根据国际乒联纪律规则和国际乒联裁决规程寻求实施一项或多项制裁。

3.5.3　精神面貌

3.5.3.1　运动员、教练员和官员应维护本项运动的良好风貌，诚实守信，避免以违反体育道德的方式来影响比赛。

3.5.3.1.1　运动员应尽力赢得比赛，除生病或受伤外，不得退出比赛。

3.5.3.1.2　运动员、教练员和官员不应参与或支持任何形式的与其比赛有关的打赌或赌博。

3.5.3.2　任何故意不遵守这些规定的运动员，将在有奖金的比赛项目中被处罚扣除全部或部分奖金，和 / 或暂停参加国际乒联的比赛。

3.5.3.3　如果任何指导者或官员被证实共同参与，相关协会也应处罚此人。

3.5.3.4　国际乒联纪律小组将对任何严重、屡次、持续违反 3.5.3 条款的行为采取进一步行动，并根据国际乒联纪律规则和国际乒联裁决规程寻求实施一项或多项制裁。

3.6　淘汰赛的抽签

3.6.1　轮空和预选赛

3.6.1.1　淘汰赛正赛的第一轮位置数应为 2 的幂。

3.6.1.1.1　如果位置数多于报名人数，第一轮应设置足够的轮空位置以补足所需位置数。

3.6.1.1.2　如果位置数少于报名人数，应举行预选赛，使通过预选赛的人数和免于参加预选赛的人数的总和等于所需的位置数。

3.6.1.2　轮空位置应按照种子排列先后次序安排，在第一轮中尽可能均匀分布。

3.6.1.3　通过预选赛的选手应视情况尽可能均匀地抽入相应的上下半区、各 1/4 区、1/8 区或 1/16 区。

3.6.2　按排名排列种子

3.6.2.1　排名在前的选手应被列为种子，以使其在比赛进行到较后轮次时相遇。

3.6.2.2　种子数不得超过该项比赛正赛第一轮的选手数。

3.6.2.3　第一号种子应安排在上半区的顶部，第二号种子应安排在下半区的底部，其余种子应通过抽签进入规定的位置，具体如下：

3.6.2.3.1　第三、第四号种子应抽入上半区的底部和下半区的顶部；

3.6.2.3.2　第五至第八号种子应抽入单数 1/4 区的底部和双数 1/4 区的顶部；

3.6.2.3.3　第九至第十六号种子应抽入单数 1/8 区的底部和双数 1/8 区的顶部；

3.6.2.3.4　第十七至第三十二号种子应抽入单数 1/16 区的底部和双数 1/16 区的顶部。

3.6.2.4　在团体淘汰赛中，每一协会中排名最高的队才有资格按排名被列为种子。

3.6.2.5　排列种子应按国际乒联最新公布的排名表为准，下列情况除外：

3.6.2.5.1　如果有资格排列为种子的报名选手（队）均来自同一洲联合会下属的协会，该联合会最新公布的排名表应优先考虑；

3.6.2.5.2　如果有资格排列为种子的报名选手均来自同一协会，该协会最新公布的排名表应优先考虑。

3.6.3　按协会提名排列种子

3.6.3.1　根据 3.6.3.3 和 3.6.3.4 条款，来自同一协会的报名选手应尽可能合理分开，除非某个项目或组别的规程中有其他具体说明。

3.6.3.2　各协会应按技术水平由强至弱排列其报名选手和双打配对的顺序，且应从包括在种子排名表内的选手开始，并应与种子排名表的顺序一致。

3.6.3.3　排列为第一和第二号的选手应被抽入不同的半区，第三和第四号选手应被抽入没有本协会第一、第二号选手所在的另外两个 1/4 区。

3.6.3.4　同协会其余选手，仅在小组赛、淘汰赛的预选赛及正赛第一轮合理分开，在后续轮次不考虑。

3.6.3.5　由不同协会的选手组成的男子双打或女子双打配对，应被视为属于在世界排名表中排名较高选手的协会；如果 2 名选手在世界排名表中无排名，则应被视为属于在相应的洲联合会排名表中排名较高选手的协会；如果 2 名选手均不在上述排名表内，则应被视为属于在世界团体赛排名表中排名较高的协会。

3.6.3.6　由不同协会的选手组成的混合双打配对，应被视为属于男选手的协会。

3.6.3.7　或者，任何由不同协会的选手组成的双打配对可被视为同属于这两个协会。

3.6.3.8　在预选赛中，同一协会的选手根据预选赛的分组数目应抽入不同的小组，并应按 3.6.3.3 和 3.6.3.4 条款所述的原则使通过预选赛的选手尽可能地合理分开。

3.6.4　变更抽签

3.6.4.1　只有竞赛管理委员会授权，才能对已经结束的抽签结果进行更改，情况许可时，还须征得各与之直接有关协会代表的同意。

3.6.4.2　只有在纠正因通知和接受报名方面产生的错误和误解，纠正 3.6.5 条款所述的严重不平衡，或按 3.6.6 条款所述增加补报的运动员时，才可对抽签结果进行更改。

3.6.4.3　一个项目比赛开始后，除必要的删减外，抽签结果不可做任何更改；就本规程而言，预选赛可视作一个单独项目。

3.6.4.4　未得到有关运动员的许可，不可将其从抽签结果中删除，除非其已被取消比赛资格。如果运动员到会，该许可应由运动员本人提出；如果运动员缺席，可由其授权的代表提出。

3.6.4.5　如果2名双打运动员均已到会，健康状况允许比赛，不得变更其配对，变更配对的理由须是其中一名运动员受伤、生病或缺席。

3.6.5　重新抽签

3.6.5.1　除3.6.4.2、3.6.4.5和3.6.5.2条款所述情况外，不允许将运动员从抽签结果的一个位置移到另一个位置。如果因任何原因使抽签结果极不平衡，应尽可能全部重新抽签。

3.6.5.2　如果不平衡是由同一抽签区内若干种子选手或配对缺席造成的，只可将剩余种子按照排名重新排列顺序，在种子位置内重新抽签，尽可能考虑按协会提名排列种子的规定。

3.6.6　增补

3.6.6.1　未包括在最初抽签结果中的运动员，由竞赛管理委员会许可及经裁判长同意，可以增补。

3.6.6.2　首先，应按排名顺序将实力最强的增补运动员补抽进种子位的空缺；将其他选手先抽入因缺席或取消资格而出现的空位，然后抽入不与种子位相邻的轮空位。

3.6.6.3　如果运动员或双打配对在最初抽签结果中按照排名可以排列为种子，则只能抽入种子位置的空缺。

3.7　竞赛的组织工作

3.7.1　许可

3.7.1.1　在遵守章程规定的前提下，任何协会都可以在本土组织或授权组织公开赛、限制赛或邀请赛或安排国际比赛。

3.7.1.2 除元老赛外，国际乒联会员协会下属的运动员，在参加国际比赛时只能通过所属协会报名参加国际乒联的比赛、国际乒联批准的比赛和在国际乒联注册的比赛，以及通过国家奥委会或国家残奥委会报名参加国际乒联认可的赛事。只有获得所属协会或国际乒联明确的书面许可，运动员才能参加其他类型的比赛；除非收到运动员所属协会或国际乒联不允许运动员参加某项赛事或系列赛事的相关通知，运动员将被视为已获参赛许可。

3.7.1.3 一个运动员或运动队如果被所属协会或洲联合会暂停比赛，将不得参加国际比赛。

3.7.1.4 未经国际乒联的允许，任何比赛不能冠以"世界"名称；未经洲联合会允许，不能冠以"洲"名称。

3.7.2 代表资格

3.7.2.1 有选手报名参加国际公开锦标赛的所有协会的代表有权出席抽签，有权参与磋商抽签的更改或可能直接影响其选手申诉的决定。

3.7.3 报名

3.7.3.1 国际公开锦标赛的报名表，应不迟于比赛开始前2个月和报名截止前1个月寄给所有协会。

3.7.3.2 公开赛的组织者应接受由协会报名参赛的所有选手，但有权安排报名选手进行预选赛；在决定此安排时，组织者应考虑国际乒联和洲联合会有关的排名，以及由报名协会提出的报名顺序。

3.7.4　比赛项目

3.7.4.1　国际公开锦标赛应包括男子单打、女子单打、男子双打、女子双打，也可包括混合双打和协会代表队之间的国际团体赛。

3.7.4.2　在冠以"世界"名称的比赛中，参加青少年项目的运动员必须在该比赛举行的前一年 12 月 31 日前不满 19 岁和 15 岁。建议在其他相应的青少年比赛中采用以下的年龄限制：21 岁以下、19 岁以下、15 岁以下、13 以下和 11 岁以下。

3.7.4.3　建议国际公开锦标赛上的团体赛应按 3.7.6 条款中的一种比赛方式进行；并在报名表或比赛指南中注明所选定的比赛方式。

3.7.4.4　单项比赛的正赛一般应采用淘汰制进行，但团体赛和单项预选赛可以按淘汰制或分组循环制进行。

3.7.5　分组循环赛

3.7.5.1　在分组循环赛中，小组里每一成员应与组内所有其他成员进行比赛；胜一场得 2 分，在完成的比赛中负一场得 1 分，因未出场或未完成比赛而负一场得 0 分；小组名次应主要根据所获得的积分决定。如果一名运动员因任何原因在一场比赛后被取消成绩，他（她）将被认为输掉该场比赛，并按照未出场比赛而负一场记录。

3.7.5.2　如果小组的 2 个或更多的成员积分相同，其有关的名次应按其相互之间比赛的成绩决定。首先计算他（她）们之间获得的积分，再根据需要计算单项比赛场次（团体赛时）、局和分的胜负比率，直至算出名次。

3.7.5.3　如果在任何阶段已经决定出一个或更多小组成员的名次后，而其他小组成员仍然得分相同，为决定相同分数成员的名次，根据 3.7.5.1 和 3.7.5.2 条款程序继续计算时，应将已决定出名次的小组成员的比赛成绩删除。

3.7.5.4　如果按照 3.7.5.1 至 3.7.5.3 条款所规定的程序，仍不能决定某些队（人）的名次时，这些队（人）的名次将由抽签来决定。

3.7.5.5　经仲裁委员会许可除外，如果小组预选一人或一队晋级，该小组的最后一场比赛应在小组排列第一和第二位的选手或队之间进行；如果小组预选两人或两队晋级，该小组的最后一场比赛应在小组排列第二和第三位的选手或队之间进行，并依此类推。

3.7.6　团体比赛形式

3.7.6.1　五场三胜制（新斯韦思林杯赛制，5 场单打）：

3.7.6.1.1　一个队由 3 名运动员组成。

3.7.6.1.2　比赛顺序是：

（1）A–X

（2）B–Y

（3）C–Z

（4）A–Y

（5）B–X

3.7.6.2　五场三胜制（考比伦杯赛制，4 场单打和 1 场双打）：

3.7.6.2.1　一个队由 2、3 或 4 名运动员组成。

3.7.6.2.2　比赛顺序是：

（1）A–X

（2）B–Y

（3）双打

（4）A–Y

（5）B–X

3.7.6.2.3　在残疾人乒乓球项目中，运动员出场顺序可参照 3.7.6.2.2，但双打比赛可以最后进行。

3.7.6.3　五场三胜制（奥林匹克赛制，4 场单打和 1 场双打）：

3.7.6.3.1　一个队由 3 名运动员组成；每名运动员最多参加 2 场单项比赛。

3.7.6.3.2　比赛顺序是：

（1）双打 B & C–Y & Z

（2）A–X

（3）C–Z

（4）A–Y

（5）B–X

3.7.6.4　七场四胜制（6 场单打和 1 场双打）：

3.7.6.4.1　一个队由 3、4 或 5 名运动员组成。

3.7.6.4.2　比赛顺序是：

（1）A–X

（2）B–Y

（3）C–Z

（4）双打

（5）A–Y

（6）C–X

（7）B–Z

3.7.6.5　九场五胜制（9 场单打）：

3.7.6.5.1　一个队由 3 名运动员组成。

3.7.6.5.2　比赛顺序是：

（1）A–X

（2）B–Y

（3）C–Z

（4）B–X

（5）A–Z

（6）C–Y

（7）B–Z

（8）C–X

（9）A–Y

3.7.7　团体比赛程序

3.7.7.1　所有出场运动员应从团体赛报名名单中挑选。

3.7.7.2　无论是否上场比赛，参赛队队长的姓名应提前向裁判员确认。

3.7.7.3　团体比赛前由抽签的中签者优先选择 A、B、C 或 X、Y、Z，由队长向裁判长或其代理人提交该队名单，并对每一名运动员确定一个字母。

3.7.7.4　双打比赛的配对可在前一场单打比赛结束时提交。

3.7.7.5　当一个队赢得足够多数的单（双）打场次时，该场团体比赛结束。

3.7.8　成绩

3.7.8.1　主办协会在比赛结束后 7 天之内，应尽快将详细成绩和比分，包括国际比赛、洲比赛和国际公开锦标赛的各轮成绩，以及全国锦标赛的最后几轮的成绩，寄给国际乒联秘书处和有关洲联合会的秘书。

3.7.9　电视和流播

3.7.9.1　除冠以世界、洲、奥运会、残奥会名称的比赛，其他比赛只有经主办协会许可，才可对比赛进行电视转播。

3.7.9.2　运动员参加一次国际比赛时，将被认为同意主办协会控制来访运动员在该比赛中的电视转播事宜；在参加世界、洲、奥运会、残奥会比赛时，运动员将被认为同意在任何地点进行比赛期间的现场直播和赛后 1 个月之内的录像播出。

3.7.9.3　国际乒联赛事（所有类别）的所有流播，须通过国际乒联流播认证程序，流播认证费（SCF）应向该赛事权利所有人收取。

3.8　国际比赛资格

3.8.1　在冠以奥林匹克名称的比赛中，参赛资格由 4.5.1 条款单独规定；在冠以残疾人奥林匹克名称的比赛中，参赛资格由国际残奥委会（IPC）及 4.6.1 条款单独规定；4.1.3、4.2.3、4.3.6、4.4.3 条款适用于世界级比赛的参赛资格。

3.8.2　如果一名运动员接受过一个协会的提名并参加了3.1.2.3 条款所列的比赛或地区锦标赛，这名运动员则被视为代表该协会，但公开锦标赛的单项比赛除外。

3.8.3　一名运动员必须拥有所代表协会所属国家的国籍，才能代表该协会参赛。但根据先前的条例已合法代表另一个协会参赛但不具有国民身份的运动员，可以保留原来的参赛资格。

3.8.3.1　当运动员属于同一国籍的不同协会，该运动员只能代表其中一个协会参赛，要么是其出生地协会，要么是其常住地协会。

3.8.3.2　如果一名运动员有资格代表一个以上协会，他（她）有权选择代表其中一个协会参赛。

3.8.4　只有当运动员根据 3.8.3 条款有资格代表洲联合会（1.3.1）的某个协会时，才能代表该洲联合会参加洲际团体比赛。

3.8.5　一名运动员在 3 年内不得代表不同协会参赛。

3.8.6　一个协会可以提名本协会所属运动员（1.8.4）参加任何国际公开锦标赛的单项比赛，这种提名可能在成绩册和国际乒联出版物中提及，但不影响该运动员根据 3.8.2 条款规定的代表资格。

3.8.7　如果裁判长要求，运动员或其协会应提供有关参赛资格的证明文件和护照。

3.8.8　任何有关资格问题的申诉应提交资格委员会，资格委员会由执行委员会、规则委员会主席和运动员委员会主席组成，该委员会的决定为最后的决定。

第四章 世界级比赛、奥运会比赛及残疾人奥运会比赛规程

4.1 世界锦标赛

4.1.1 组织的权力

4.1.1.1 世界锦标赛，本部分简称"锦标赛"，为国际乒联代表大会指定锦标赛设立项目并委托某协会承办的比赛。

4.1.1.2 申请举办锦标赛的截止日期由国际乒联执行委员会确定，并至少在 6 个月前通告所有的协会。

4.1.1.3 所有申请均应由国际乒联执行委员会审核，并与遴选委员会的报告一起送交国际乒联代表大会，如果可以，应包括届时相关场馆的报告。

4.1.1.4 如有必要，国际乒联代表大会或执行委员会可要求一个或几个相关的委员会成员去申办协会考察，以确信申办方提出的比赛和其他安排是否适当，考察的费用由该协会承担。

4.1.1.5 主办协会确定下来后，如果情况发生变化并可能影响到比赛的顺利举办时，则赛前一届的国际乒联代表大会可以 2/3 的多数票推翻主办权；在两个代表大会召开之间，理事会有权决定将锦标赛改在异地或采取其他适当行动。

4.1.2   主办协会的职责

4.1.2.1   协会一旦获准举办锦标赛，就称为"主办协会"。主办协会应该根据《乒乓球规则》、《乒乓球国际竞赛规程》和《世界比赛规程》，以及由理事会授权修改和补充的竞赛指南组织比赛。

4.1.2.2   主办协会应该从锦标赛开始前一天中午起，到比赛结束的第二天上午为止，为下列人员提供食宿：

4.1.2.2.1   一个协会指定的参赛人员，最多不超过 2 名男运动员和 2 名女运动员；

4.1.2.2.2   每个协会 1 名参加国际乒联代表大会的代表，如其姓名不在上述指定的运动员之列；

4.1.2.2.3   国际乒联执行委员会、理事会和洲理事会的成员，其他委员会正式成员及技术和性别专员；

4.1.2.2.4   由运动科学与医疗委员会指定的兴奋剂检测监督员，最多 3 人；

4.1.2.2.5   未包含在运动员报名单中的运动员委员会成员；

4.1.2.2.6   名誉主席；

4.1.2.2.7   个人名誉委员；

4.1.2.2.8   主席顾问委员会成员；

4.1.2.2.9   根据国际乒联世界级比赛中竞赛官员指南所邀请的其他协会的国际级裁判员、裁判长和考官；

4.1.2.2.10   国际乒联工作人员，最多 7 人（包含 1 名协助兴奋剂检测监督员）。

4.1.2.3   如果国际乒联的业务工作超过锦标赛的时间，主办协会应相应延长对参加该业务的人员的食宿招待。

4.1.2.4   主办协会将为所有参赛者免费提供医疗和药品，但是建议每个协会为其参赛队员和官员在锦标赛期间投保疾病和伤害险。

4.1.2.5　主办协会应负担参赛者往返驻地与比赛场馆间的交通费用。

4.1.2.6　主办协会应要求本国政府免收所有参赛者的签证费。

4.1.2.7　主办协会应确保所有的运动员、官员以及 4.1.2.2 条款所列的人员、编外运动员、委员会成员以及国际乒联任命的翻译、医生或医疗顾问可自由出入赛场。

4.1.2.8　主办协会应提供至少 4 种语言的、一流的翻译服务，最好有相应设备支持的同声传译。

4.1.2.9　主办协会应在锦标赛场馆内为国际乒联提供办公室，配备翻译、计算机、互联网、电话、传真和复印设备供其使用。

4.1.2.10　主办协会应该发行一份比赛指南，详细介绍锦标赛的组织情况，内容包括：

4.1.2.10.1　锦标赛的日期和地点；

4.1.2.10.2　锦标赛举办的项目；

4.1.2.10.3　锦标赛使用的器材；

4.1.2.10.4　锦标赛的报名程序、报名费以及所需承诺；

4.1.2.10.5　抽签的日期和地点；

4.1.2.10.6　仲裁会议和代表大会的日期；

4.1.2.10.7　运动员和官员的接待范围；

4.1.2.10.8　任何由理事会授权对锦标赛颁发的指令。

4.1.2.11　在锦标赛期间，主办协会应及时为国际乒联执行委员会成员、理事会成员和各队的领队提供包括详细比分的比赛成绩；比赛结束后，主办协会应尽快公布包括详细比分的整套成绩册，并分发给所有协会。

4.1.3　资格

4.1.3.1　只有未拖欠会费（1.7.3.3），且在世界锦标赛前的洲锦标赛（包括预选赛）或洲运动会中至少有一名运动员或运动队报名参赛的协会，才有资格在世界锦标赛中为其运动员或运动队报名。

4.1.3.2　除规则 3.8 条款的规定外，获得新国籍并希望代表该国籍对应协会的运动员，应通过新协会向国际乒联注册。该运动员注册日期为国际乒联运动员注册确认之日或该运动员获得其新国籍之日（以较早者为准）。

4.1.3.3　运动员在下列情况下不能代表新协会：

4.1.3.3.1　如果运动员注册时年龄未满 15 岁，自注册之日起未满 3 年，或者该运动员从未代表过其他协会，但自注册之日起未满 1 年；

4.1.3.3.2　如果运动员注册时年满 15 岁但未到 18 岁，自注册之日起未满 5 年；

4.1.3.3.3　如果运动员注册时年满 18 岁但未到 21 岁，自注册之日起未满 7 年；

4.1.3.3.4　如果运动员注册时已年满 21 岁，自注册之日起未满 9 年。

4.1.3.4　曾经参加过世界锦标赛的运动员，将保留其参赛资格。

4.1.4　报名费

4.1.4.1　团体比赛每支球队的报名费为 100 美元，每对双打为 50 美元，每名单打为 25 美元。

4.1.4.2　参赛协会在报名时应该向主办协会缴纳报名费，报名费由主办协会和国际乒联均分。

4.1.4.3　　每一个报名的协会都应按时缴纳报名费，除了因不可控制的原因而不能参加锦标赛的协会，理事会可免除其报名费。

4.1.5　　递交报名表

4.1.5.1　　有意向派球队或队员参加锦标赛的协会，应通过填写秘书处提供的预报名表告知国际乒联。接收预报名表的截止日期最晚不超过锦标赛开始前 4 个月。

4.1.5.2　　报名信息由竞赛部连同竞赛指南一并发布，报名表应按要求提交。

4.1.5.3　　最终报名的提交截止日期应不晚于锦标赛开始前的 2 个月。

4.1.5.4　　团体比赛，每个协会可报名最多 5 名运动员和 1 名不参赛的队长。如果没有任命不参赛的队长，将从 5 名运动员中指定 1 名担任队长。

4.1.5.5　　各协会应按技术水平对报名的运动员和双打配对进行排序，排序应与他们现有的世界排名一致。

4.1.5.6　　国际乒联只接受有参赛资格协会的正式报名，报名表必须由协会负责人签名，并在截止日期当日或之前被收到。

4.1.6　　报名的更改

4.1.6.1　　主办协会可以接受对报名的更改，但应由报名协会的 1 名代表在锦标赛首次正式抽签日期前一天的任何时间上报（适用于单项比赛）。

4.1.6.2　　报名协会可以改变团体阵容的组成，但必须在锦标赛前召开的仲裁会议之前向主办协会提出。此截止日期之后，不接受任何进一步的更改。

4.1.6.3　由于任何错误或缺席原因而请求更改抽签的协会，其代表抵达锦标赛场馆就应向裁判长或副裁判长告知，或确认已经通告过的改动，需使用（填写）为更改报名而准备的表格。

4.1.6.4　仅考虑由协会代表在抵达赛场就立即提出或确认的报名更改。除非因为后来队员的缺席，双打配对中 1 名运动员生病或者受伤，此类情况应在突发出现时立即提出更改要求。

4.1.6.5　所有经过许可的更改应该立即通知各队队长，并在可能的情况下通知参赛协会代表。

4.1.7　报名须知

4.1.7.1　报名表应包括一个声明，该声明由参赛协会负责人代表提名的运动员和队长签署，表明他们理解和接受锦标赛的条件，愿意与所有其他参赛队 / 队员进行比赛。没有该声明，报名表无效。

4.1.7.2　单项比赛中，所有的参赛者都被视为个人选手；无论其他的参赛对手是否来自同一协会，运动员都应尽最大努力赢得所有参加的比赛，并且不能退出比赛，除非受伤或生病。

4.1.8　仲裁委员会

4.1.8.1　仲裁委员会应该包括技术专员、技术委员会主席、规则委员会主席、裁判员和裁判长委员会主席、竞赛部 1 名代表、组委会 1 名代表和裁判长。裁判长有发言权，但无投票权。

4.1.8.2　如果以上任何 1 名指定的主席无法出席仲裁会议，他（她）可以提名其所在委员会的其他成员出席，该成员有发言权和投票权。

4.1.8.3　　仲裁委员会的主席由仲裁委员会成员指定。

4.1.8.4　　任何受仲裁会议正在审议事项直接影响的协会，应有权派代表出席仲裁会议，但无权投票。

4.1.8.5　　仲裁委员会有权对在竞赛管理委员会管辖范围内的任何申诉做出裁决，可批准团体阵容的变动。

4.1.8.6　　仲裁委员会应在锦标赛开始前召开仲裁会议，了解当时提出的所有抽签变更请求，对各队阵容的变动申请做出决定；抽签变更的任何后续问题将由技术专员配合竞赛部代表共同做出决定，仅当出现对其行政决定或裁判长的决定提出申诉时，仲裁委员会主席将再次召开仲裁会议。

4.1.9　　竞赛项目

4.1.9.1　　在偶数年份，锦标赛将举行男子团体、女子团体比赛；而在奇数年份，锦标赛将举行男子单打、女子单打、男子双打、女子双打和混合双打比赛。

4.1.9.2　　双打比赛中，配对运动员可以来自不同的协会。

4.1.9.3　　团体和单项比赛的赛制、团体预选赛的比赛方法及实施日期应由技术专员及竞赛部提出建议，由理事会决定。

4.1.9.4　　团体比赛按照3.7.6.1条款规定应为5场3胜的单打比赛。

4.1.9.5　　单打比赛的第一轮，不能超过128个位置；男子、女子、混合双打比赛第一轮，不能超过64个位置，除非得到执行委员会的另外许可。

4.1.9.6　　每个协会可报名3名男运动员和3名女运动员参加每项单打比赛，可增报在锦标赛当年1月份国际乒联公布的世界排名前100的运动员1名，增报世界排名前

20 的运动员 1 名，但总数不能超过 5 名男运动员和 5 名女运动员。每个协会最多可报 4 名男运动员参加男双比赛，4 名女运动员参加女双比赛，以及 2 名男运动员和 2 名女运动员参加混双比赛；各项目的运动员可以不同，但每个协会每个双打项目最多只能报 2 对组合配对（运动员来自不同的协会）。

4.1.9.6.1　无论排名如何，主办协会最多可报 6 名男运动员和 6 名女运动员参加单打、3 对男子双打、3 对女子双打和 3 对混合双打比赛。

4.1.9.7　来自同一协会的运动员，根据 3.6.3.1 条款规定，仅在预选赛的轮次和分组赛以及正赛第一轮中合理分开，后续轮次不再考虑。

4.1.10　缺席

4.1.10.1　进入团体抽签的队，无充分正当理由未参加比赛，该协会将受到国际乒联代表大会的纪律处罚。

4.1.10.2　一个队指定参加团体比赛的队员应自始至终完成每场团体比赛，除非裁判长确信缺席是由于意外、生病、受伤或其他运动员或协会无法控制的情况，裁判长可允许团体赛中的一名队员缺席，或免去一场比赛，包括裁判长在其职权范围内取消比赛资格的判罚。

4.1.10.3　如果一个队在团体比赛中，未完成计划的比赛，该协会代表在锦标赛的免费招待可被取消。协会对此可向仲裁委员会提出申诉，仲裁委员会的决定将是最终的决定。

4.1.11　兴奋剂检测

4.1.11.1　兴奋剂检测应按照国际乒联反兴奋剂条例执行。

4.1.12　　　奖励和仪式

4.1.12.1　　锦标赛永久性的奖杯是：

4.1.12.1.1　男子团体斯韦思林杯；

4.1.12.1.2　女子团体考比伦杯；

4.1.12.1.3　男子单打圣·勃莱德杯；

4.1.12.1.4　女子单打吉·盖斯特杯；

4.1.12.1.5　男子双打伊朗杯；

4.1.12.1.6　女子双打波普杯；

4.1.12.1.7　混合双打赫杜塞克杯。

4.1.12.2　　团体冠军获胜的协会，单项冠军获胜的个人，将保留相应的奖杯直至夺冠次年的 12 月 31 日；双打冠军获胜的配对，可约定或抽签决定保留奖杯指定期限一半的顺序。

4.1.12.3　　连续三届或总共四次获得男子或女子单打冠军的运动员，将得到国际乒联相应奖杯一半尺寸的复制品作为纪念（永久拥有）。

4.1.12.4　　团体和单项比赛，在决赛中获胜的运动员将获得金牌，在决赛中失利的运动员将获得银牌，在半决赛中失利的运动员将获得铜牌。

4.1.12.5　　团体和单项比赛的颁奖仪式，应悬挂金牌、银牌和铜牌获得者国家的国旗，奏金牌获得者国家的国歌。

4.1.12.6　　获得团体或单项奖杯的协会，应书面确认收到奖杯，并在指定期限临近时，在秘书处通知的 14 天内，将奖杯在约定的时间内送到约定的地点。

4.1.12.7　　确认收到奖杯的协会应负责妥善保管奖杯，包括为奖杯投保。保险费用和胜者名字（团体比赛应包括不参赛队长的名字）刻字费用由获胜者所属协会承担。

4.1.12.8　如果协会在保管奖杯期间将奖杯丢失，该协会有责任提供相似的复制品。

4.1.12.9　在闭幕式上，作为锦标赛友谊象征的埃及杯将传递给下一届锦标赛举办城市的代表，该城市将保留埃及杯直至下届锦标赛。

4.1.13　商业权利

4.1.13.1　国际乒联在全球范围内独家享有和控制锦标赛及相关的所有商业权利。该商业权利包括但不限于在以下所有方面：

4.1.13.1.1　音频、视频、音视频及数据版权（存于每种媒介，无论在这些条款发布之日是否存在）；

4.1.13.1.2　赞助、广告、销售、市场推广及其他形式的结社权；

4.1.13.1.3　票务、接待及其他特许经营权；

4.1.13.1.4　锦标赛商业化的其他权利（包括但不限于任何所谓"赛事权"和任何授权对锦标赛进行投注的权利）。

4.1.13.2　国际乒联有权以其认为适当的方式开发其商业权利，包括不定期地给相关的协会或其他第三方发放同等（或部分）权利许可证。

4.1.13.3　每个协会应确保其成员（官员、运动员、代表和其他隶属机构）做到：

4.1.13.3.1　完全遵守任何及所有的规则、规程，以及由国际乒联或其代表不定期颁发的与商业权利开发相关的指南；

4.1.13.3.2　提供所要求的权利、设施和服务以确保国际乒联和／或相关第三方得以在开发任何商业权利的合约下履行其义务，并且不得以任何作为或者不作为侵犯根据本协议授予的任何独家权利，或以其他方式造成违约。为避免疑义，只有国际乒联可针对某协会强制执行此规则，没有第三方有权这样做。

4.2　世界青年锦标赛

4.2.1　组织的权力

4.2.1.1　世界青年锦标赛，本部分简称"锦标赛"，为国际乒联代表大会指定锦标赛设立项目并委托某协会承办的比赛。

4.2.1.2　申请举办锦标赛截止日期由执行委员会确定，并至少在 6 个月前通知所有协会。国际乒联只接受下 2 届锦标赛的举办申请。

4.2.1.3　所有申请应由执行委员会审核，并连同届时相关场馆的详细信息送交理事会。

4.2.1.4　如有必要，理事会或执行委员会可要求青少年专员去申办协会考察，以确信申办方提出的比赛和其他安排是否适当，考察的费用由该协会承担。

4.2.1.5　主办协会确定下来后，如果情况发生变化并有可能影响到比赛的顺利举办时，则赛前一届的国际乒联代表大会可以 2/3 的多数票推翻主办权；在 2 个代表大会召开之间，理事会有权决定将锦标赛改在异地或采取其他适当行动。

4.2.2　主办协会的职责

4.2.2.1　协会一旦获准举办锦标赛，就称为"主办协会"。主办协会应该根据《乒乓球规则》、《乒乓球国际竞赛规程》和《世界青年锦标赛规程》，以及由理事会授权修改和补充的竞赛指南组织比赛。

4.2.2.2   主办协会应该从锦标赛开始前一天中午起，到比赛结束的第二天上午为止，为下列人员提供食宿：

4.2.2.2.1   参赛协会指定有资格参加青年男子团体比赛的运动员，人数不超过 2 名；

4.2.2.2.2   参赛协会指定有资格参加青年女子团体比赛的运动员，人数不超过 2 名；

4.2.2.2.3   参加 1 个或 2 个团体项目的协会不超过 1 名教练员；

4.2.2.2.4   国际乒联执行委员会成员和青少年专员；

4.2.2.2.5   由运动科学与医疗委员会指定的兴奋剂检测监督员，最多 2 名；

4.2.2.2.6   由执行委员会任命的国际乒联各委员会主席或专员，最多 2 名；

4.2.2.2.7   根据国际乒联世界级比赛中竞赛官员指南所邀请的其他协会的国际级裁判员、裁判长和考官；

4.2.2.2.8   最多 7 名国际乒联工作人员。

4.2.2.3   主办协会将为所有参赛者免费提供医疗和药品，但是建议每个协会为其参赛队员和官员在锦标赛期间投保疾病和伤害险。

4.2.2.4   主办协会应负担参赛者往返驻地与比赛场馆间的交通费用。

4.2.2.5   主办协会应要求本国政府免收所有参赛者的签证费。

4.2.2.6   主办协会应确保所有的运动员、官员以及 4.2.2.2 条款所列的人员、编外运动员、委员会成员以及国际乒联任命的翻译、医生或医疗顾问可自由进出比赛场馆及相关区域。

4.2.2.7	主办协会应在场馆内为国际乒联提供办公室，配备翻译、计算机、互联网、电话、传真和复印设备供其使用。
4.2.2.8	主办协会应该发行一份比赛指南，详细介绍锦标赛的组织情况，内容包括：
4.2.2.8.1	锦标赛的日期和地点；
4.2.2.8.2	锦标赛举办的项目；
4.2.2.8.3	锦标赛使用的器材；
4.2.2.8.4	锦标赛的报名程序、报名费以及所需承诺；
4.2.2.8.5	抽签的日期和地点；
4.2.2.8.6	仲裁会议的日期；
4.2.2.8.7	运动员和官员的接待范围；
4.2.2.8.8	任何由理事会授权对锦标赛颁发的指令。
4.2.2.9	在锦标赛期间，主办协会应及时为国际乒联执行委员会成员、理事会成员和各队的领队提供包括详细比分的比赛成绩；比赛结束后，主办协会应尽快公布包括详细比分的整套成绩册，并分发给所有协会。

4.2.3　资格

4.2.3.1	只有未拖欠会费的协会（1.7.3.3）才有资格为运动队或运动员个人报名参加锦标赛。
4.2.3.2	团体和单项的预选赛比赛方式，将由理事会在锦标赛开赛前 18 个月做出决定。
4.2.3.3	根据规则 3.7.4.2 条款的规定，所有运动员必须在 19 岁以下和 15 岁以下。
4.2.3.4	除规则 3.8 条款的规定外，获得新国籍并希望代表该国籍对应协会的运动员，应通过新协会向国际乒联注册。该运动员注册日期为国际乒联运动员注册确认之

日或该运动员获得新国籍之日（以较早者为准）。

4.2.3.5　如果运动员注册时未满 15 岁，则该运动员在注册之日起 3 年内不得代表新的协会；如该运动员从未代表过其他协会，则自注册之日起 1 年内不得代表新的协会。

4.2.3.6　注册时已满 15 岁的运动员，不得在锦标赛中代表新的协会，除了曾经参加过世界青年 / 青少年锦标赛的运动员，将保留其参赛资格。

4.2.4　报名费

4.2.4.1　团体比赛每支球队的报名费为 50 美元，每对双打为 30 美元，每名单打为 15 美元。

4.2.4.2　参赛协会在报名时应该向主办协会缴纳报名费，报名费由主办协会和国际乒联均分。

4.2.4.3　每一个报名的协会都应按时缴纳报名费，除了因不可控制的原因而不能参加锦标赛的协会，理事会可免除其报名费。

4.2.5　资格和报名

4.2.5.1　有资格派运动队或运动员参加锦标赛的协会，应通过填写秘书处提供的预报名表告知主办方和国际乒联其参赛意向。接收预报名表的截止日期最晚不超过锦标赛开始前 4 个月。

4.2.5.2　报名信息由竞赛部连同竞赛指南一并发布，报名表应按照要求提交。

4.2.5.3　2 份报名表返还主办协会，1 份报名表返还秘书处。收到报名表的截止日期不晚于锦标赛开始前的 2 个月。

4.2.5.4　各协会应按技术水平对报名的运动员和双打配对进行排序，排序应与其现有的世界青少年排名一致。

4.2.5.5　　主办协会只接受有参赛资格协会的正式报名，报名表必须由协会负责人签名，并在截止日期当日或之前被收到。

4.2.6　　**报名的更改**

4.2.6.1　　报名协会可以改变团体阵容的组成，但必须在锦标赛前召开的仲裁会议之前向主办协会提出。比赛一旦开始，就不能更改团体名单。

4.2.6.2　　由于任何错误或缺席原因而请求更改抽签的协会，其代表抵达锦标赛场馆就应向裁判长或副裁判长告知，或确认已经通告过的改动，需使用（填写）为更改报名而准备的表格。

4.2.6.3　　仅考虑由协会代表在抵达赛场就立即提出或确认的报名更改。除非因为后来队员的缺席，双打配对中 1 名运动员生病或者受伤，此类情况应在突发出现时立即提出更改要求。

4.2.6.4　　所有经过许可的更改应立即通知各队队长或在可能的情况下通知参赛协会代表。

4.2.7　　**报名须知**

4.2.7.1　　报名表应包括一个声明，该声明由参赛协会负责人代表指派的运动员和队长签署，表明他们理解和接受锦标赛的条件，准备与其他所有参赛队 / 队员进行比赛。没有该声明，报名表无效。

4.2.7.2　　单项比赛中，所有的参赛者都被视为个人选手；无论其他的参赛对手是否来自同一协会，运动员都应尽最大努力赢得所有参加的比赛，并且不能退出比赛，除非受伤或生病。

4.2.8 仲裁委员会

4.2.8.1 仲裁委员会应包括国际乒联青少年专员、国际乒联竞赛部代表 1 名、国际乒联全球青少年项目的代表 1 名、锦标赛主任［或他（她）的同级］、组委会代表 1 名和裁判长，裁判长有发言权，但无投票权。

4.2.8.2 如果国际乒联青少年专员无法出席仲裁会议，他（她）可以委任 1 名代表替他（她）出席，该代表有发言权和投票权。

4.2.8.3 仲裁委员会主席由国际乒联青少年专员指定。如果他（她）缺席，应由国际乒联全球青少年项目的代表重新指定。

4.2.8.4 任何受仲裁会议正在审议事项直接影响的协会，应有权派代表出席仲裁会议，但无权投票。

4.2.8.5 仲裁委员会有权对在竞赛管理委员会管辖范围内的任何申诉做出裁决。

4.2.8.6 仲裁委员会应在锦标赛开始前召开仲裁会议，了解当时提出的所有抽签变更请求；抽签变更的任何后续问题将由国际乒联青少年专员做出决定，仅当出现对其行政决定或裁判长的决定提出申诉时，国际乒联青少年专员将再次召开仲裁会议。

4.2.9 竞赛项目

4.2.9.1 锦标赛包括青年男子团体、女子团体，青年男子单、双打，青年女子单、双打和混合双打比赛。

4.2.9.2 团体和单项比赛的比赛方式和预选方式，应由理事会根据青少年专员、技术委员和竞赛部的建议做出决定，并在锦标赛开始前 6 个月通告所有协会。

4.2.10　缺席

4.2.10.1　进入团体抽签的队，无充分正当理由未参加比赛，该协会将受到国际乒联代表大会的纪律处罚。

4.2.10.2　一个队指定参加团体比赛的队员应自始至终完成每场团体比赛，除非裁判长确信缺席是由于意外、生病、受伤或其他运动员或协会无法控制的情况，裁判长可允许团体赛中的 1 名队员缺席，或免去 1 场比赛，包括裁判长在其职权范围内取消比赛资格的判罚。

4.2.10.3　如果一个队在团体比赛中，未完成计划的比赛，该协会代表在锦标赛的免费招待可被取消。协会对此可向仲裁委员会提出申诉，仲裁委员会的决定将是最终的决定。

4.2.11　兴奋剂检测

4.2.11.1　兴奋剂检测应按照国际乒联反兴奋剂条例执行。

4.2.12　奖励和仪式

4.2.12.1　团体和单项比赛，在决赛中获胜的运动员将获得金牌，在决赛中失利的运动员将获得银牌，在半决赛中失利的运动员将获得铜牌。

4.2.12.2　团体和单项比赛的颁奖仪式，应悬挂金牌、银牌和铜牌获得者国家的国旗，奏金牌获得者国家的国歌。

4.2.13　商业权利

4.2.13.1　国际乒联在全球范围内独家享有和控制锦标赛及相关的所有商业权利。该商业权利包括但不限于在以下所有方面：

4.2.13.1.1　音频、视频、音视频及数据版权（存于每种媒介，无论在这些条款发布之日是否存在）；

4.2.13.1.2　赞助、广告、销售、市场推广及其他形式的结社权；

4.2.13.1.3　票务、接待及其他特许经营权；

4.2.13.1.4　锦标赛商业化的其他权利（包括但不限于任何所谓"赛事权"和任何授权对锦标赛进行投注的权利）。

4.2.13.2　国际乒联有权以其认为适当的方式开发其商业权利，包括不定期地给相关的协会或其他第三方发放同等（或部分）权利许可证。

4.2.13.3　每个协会应确保其成员（官员、运动员、代表和其他隶属机构）做到：

4.2.13.3.1　完全遵守任何及所有的规则、规程，以及由国际乒联或其代表不定期颁发的与商业权利开发相关的指南；

4.2.13.3.2　提供所要求的权利、设施和服务以确保国际乒联和/或相关第三方得以在开发任何商业权利的合约下履行其义务，并且不得以任何作为或者不作为侵犯根据本协议授予的任何独家权利，或以其他方式造成违约。为避免疑义，只有国际乒联可针对某协会强制执行此规则，没有第三方有权这样做。

4.3　世界杯

4.3.1　组成

4.3.1.1　男子世界杯和女子世界杯应每年或每2年（偶数年）举行，世界杯大洲赛或同等级比赛应作为世界杯的预选赛。预选赛及其比赛方式是国际乒联赛历的一个组成部分。

4.3.1.2　提供参赛运动员从比赛开始的前一天晚上，到比赛结束的第二天上午的免费食宿。同时提供各洲代表前往比赛场馆所在地的免费往返机票。

4.3.2　权力

4.3.2.1　国际乒联独家享有"世界杯"这个名称及比赛的权利。

4.3.2.2　一个协会可获准举办世界杯赛。递交申请就意味着理解并接受以上所有可适用的规程。

4.3.2.3　没有国际乒联的事先批准，主办方不能将权力委托他人，也不能与任何机构，比如地方协会、市政当局或赞助商签订任何合同或协议。

4.3.2.4　主办方和其他机构达成的任何协议，既不能背离也不能贬损本条例的原则；如果出现争议，国际乒联通过其代表所行使的权力为最高权力。

4.3.2.5　国际乒联可以与推广商或赞助商签订协议。

4.3.3　任命

4.3.3.1　每次比赛，国际乒联竞赛部应指派 1 名竞赛主任和 1 名竞赛经理。

4.3.3.2　竞赛主任应对国际乒联竞赛部负责，保证比赛条件符合赛事要求，包括批准主办方对仪式、社交活动的礼仪、座位和比赛展示的安排。

4.3.3.3　竞赛经理应对国际乒联负责，确保比赛器材和比赛条件适当，监督抽签编排和安排比赛日程。

4.3.4　兴奋剂检测

4.3.4.1　兴奋剂检测应按照国际乒联反兴奋剂条例执行。

4.3.5　比赛方法

4.3.5.1　比赛方法由执行委员会根据竞赛部的建议做出决定。在对选定的运动员及其协会发出邀请的同时，应在指南中告知参赛者所采用的比赛方法。

4.3.6　　资格

4.3.6.1　　除规则 3.8 条款的规定外，获得新国籍并希望代表该国籍对应协会的运动员，应通过新协会向国际乒联注册。该运动员注册日期为国际乒联运动员注册确认之日或该运动员获得其新国籍之日（以较早者为准）。

4.3.6.2　　运动员在下列情况下不能代表新协会：

4.3.6.2.1　如果运动员注册时年龄未满 15 岁，自注册之日起未满 3 年，或者该运动员从未代表过其他协会，但自注册之日起未满 1 年；

4.3.6.2.2　如果运动员注册时年满 15 岁但未到 18 岁，自注册之日起未满 5 年；

4.3.6.2.3　如果运动员注册时年满 18 岁但未到 21 岁，自注册之日起未满 7 年；

4.3.6.2.4　如果运动员注册时已年满 21 岁，自注册之日起未满 9 年；

4.3.6.3　　曾经参加过世界杯的运动员，将保留其参赛资格。

4.3.7　　仲裁委员会

4.3.7.1　　仲裁委员会应包括国际乒联负责世界杯的执行副主席、国际乒联竞赛主任、组委会代表 1 名和裁判长。裁判长有发言权，但无投票权。

4.3.7.2　　如果国际乒联负责世界杯的执行副主席或者国际乒联竞赛主任无法出席仲裁会议，他（她）可以委任一名代表替他（她）出席，该代表有发言权和投票权。

4.3.7.3　　仲裁委员会的主席将由国际乒联负责世界杯的执行副主席指定。

4.3.7.4　　任何受仲裁会议正在审议事项直接影响的协会，应有权派代表出席仲裁会议，但无权投票。

4.3.7.5　仲裁委员会有权对在竞赛管理委员会管辖范围内就任何问题的申诉做出裁决。

4.3.7.6　仲裁委员会应在比赛开始前召开仲裁会议，了解当时提出的所有抽签变更请求。仅当出现对其行政决定或裁判长的决定提出申诉时，仲裁委员会将再次召开仲裁会议。

4.3.8　商业权利

4.3.8.1　国际乒联在全球范围内独家享有和控制锦标赛及相关的所有商业权利。该商业权利包括但不限于在以下所有方面：

4.3.8.1.1　音频、视频、音视频及数据版权（存于每种媒介，无论在这些条款发布之日是否存在）；

4.3.8.1.2　赞助、广告、销售、市场推广及其他形式的结社权；

4.3.8.1.3　票务、接待及其他特许经营权；

4.3.8.1.4　锦标赛商业化的其他权利（包括但不限于任何所谓"赛事权"和任何授权对锦标赛进行投注的权利）。

4.3.8.2　国际乒联有权以其认为适当的方式开发其商业权利，包括不定期地给相关的协会或其他第三方发放同等（或部分）权利许可证。

4.3.8.3　每个协会应确保其成员（官员、运动员、代表和其他隶属机构）做到：

4.3.8.3.1　完全遵守任何及所有的规则、规程，以及由国际乒联或其代表不定期颁发的与商业权利开发相关的指南；

4.3.8.3.2　提供所要求的权利、设施和服务以确保国际乒联和／或相关第三方得以在开发任何商业权利的合约下履行其义务，并且不得以任何作为或者不作为侵犯根据本协议授予的任何独家权利，或以其他方式造成违约。为避免疑义，只有国际乒联可针对某协会强制执行此规则，没有第三方有权这样做。

4.4 团体世界杯

4.4.1 组成

4.4.1.1 团体世界杯每 2 年（奇数年）举行，将邀请各洲团体冠军参赛。预选赛及其比赛方式是国际乒联赛历的一个组成部分。

4.4.1.2 如果主办协会的参赛队在上一届世界团体锦标赛中通过排名获得参赛资格，则上一届世界团体锦标赛排名第 8 的队伍将入选。

4.4.1.3 提供参赛运动员从比赛开始的前一天晚上，到比赛结束的第二天上午的免费食宿。

4.4.2 权力

4.4.2.1 国际乒联独家享有"团体世界杯"这个名称及比赛的权利。

4.4.2.2 一个协会可获准举办团体世界杯赛。递交申请就意味着理解并接受以上所有可适用的规程。

4.4.2.3 没有国际乒联的事先批准，主办方不能将权力委托他人，也不能与任何机构，比如地方协会、市政当局或赞助商签订任何合同或协议。

4.4.2.4 主办方和其他机构达成的任何协议，既不能背离也不能贬损本条例的原则；如果出现争议，国际乒联通过其代表所行使的权力为最高权力。

4.4.2.5　　　国际乒联可以与推广商或赞助商签订协议。

4.4.3　　　任命

4.4.3.1　　　每次比赛，国际乒联竞赛部应指派 1 名竞赛主任和 1
　　　　　　　名竞赛经理。

4.4.3.2　　　竞赛主任应对国际乒联竞赛部负责，保证比赛条件符
　　　　　　　合赛事要求，包括批准主办方对仪式、社交活动的礼
　　　　　　　仪座位和比赛展示的安排。

4.4.3.3　　　竞赛经理应对国际乒联负责，确保比赛器材和比赛条
　　　　　　　件适当，监督抽签编排和安排比赛日程。

4.4.4　　　兴奋剂检测

4.4.4.1　　　兴奋剂检测应按照国际乒联反兴奋剂条例执行。

4.4.5　　　比赛方法

4.4.5.1　　　比赛方法由执行委员会根据竞赛部的建议做出决定。
　　　　　　　在对选定的运动员及其协会发出邀请的同时，应在指
　　　　　　　南中告知参赛者所采用的比赛方法。

4.4.6　　　资格

4.4.6.1　　　除规则 3.8 条款的规定外，获得新国籍并希望代表该
　　　　　　　国籍对应协会的运动员，应通过新协会向国际乒联注
　　　　　　　册。该运动员注册日期为国际乒联运动员注册确认之
　　　　　　　日或该运动员获得其新国籍之日（以较早者为准）。

4.4.6.2　　　运动员在下列情况下不能代表新协会：

4.4.6.2.1　　如果运动员注册时年龄未满 15 岁，自注册之日起未满
　　　　　　　3 年，或者该运动员从未代表过其他协会，但自注册
　　　　　　　之日起未满 1 年；

4.4.6.2.2　　如果运动员注册时年满 15 岁但未到 18 岁，自注册之
　　　　　　　日起未满 5 年；

4.4.6.2.3	如果运动员注册时年满 18 岁但未到 21 岁，自注册之日起未满 7 年；
4.4.6.2.4	如果运动员注册时已年满 21 岁，自注册之日起未满 9 年；
4.4.6.3	曾经参加过团体世界杯的运动员，将保留其参赛资格。

4.4.7　仲裁委员会

4.4.7.1	仲裁委员会应包括国际乒联负责团体世界杯的执行副主席、国际乒联竞赛主任、组委会代表 1 名和裁判长。裁判长有发言权，但无投票权。
4.4.7.2	如果国际乒联负责团体世界杯的执行副主席或者国际乒联竞赛主任无法出席仲裁会议，他（她）可以委任一名代表替他（她）出席，该代表有发言权和投票权。
4.4.7.3	仲裁委员会的主席将由国际乒联负责团体世界杯的执行副主席指定。
4.4.7.4	任何受仲裁会议正在审议事项直接影响的协会，应有权派代表出席仲裁会议，但无权投票。
4.4.7.5	仲裁委员会有权对在竞赛管理委员会管辖范围内就任何问题的申诉做出裁决并可批准参赛队伍的变动。
4.4.7.6	仲裁委员会应在比赛开始前召开仲裁会议，了解当时提出的所有抽签变更请求。仅当出现对其行政决定或裁判长的决定提出申诉时，仲裁委员会将再次召开仲裁会议。

4.4.8　商业权利

4.4.8.1	国际乒联在全球范围内独家享有和控制锦标赛及相关的所有商业权利。该商业权利包括但不限于在以下所有方面：

4.4.8.1.1　音频、视频、音视频及数据版权（存于每种媒介，**无论在这些条款发布之日是否存在**）；

4.4.8.1.2　赞助、广告、销售、市场推广及其他形式的**结社权**；

4.4.8.1.3　票务、接待及其他特许经营权；

4.4.8.1.4　锦标赛商业化的其他权利（包括但不限于任何所谓"赛事权"和任何授权对锦标赛进行投注的权利）。

4.4.8.2　国际乒联有权以其认为适当的方式开发其商业权利，包括不定期地给相关的协会或其他第三方发放同等（或部分）权利许可证。

4.4.8.3　每个协会应确保其成员（官员、运动员、代表和其他隶属机构）做到：

4.4.8.3.1　完全遵守任何及所有的规则、规程，以及由国际乒联或其代表不定期颁发的与商业权利开发相关的指南；

4.4.8.3.2　提供所要求的权利、设施和服务以确保国际乒联和 /或相关第三方得以在开发任何商业权利的合约下履行其义务，并且不得以任何作为或者不作为侵犯根据本协议授予的任何独家权利，或以其他方式造成违约。为避免疑义，只有国际乒联可针对某协会强制执行此规则，没有第三方有权这样做。

4.5　奥运会比赛

4.5.1　资格

4.5.1.1　有资格参加奥运会的运动员、教练员或官员，应遵守《奥林匹克宪章》和国际乒联规则。以上人员还应该是：

4.5.1.1.1　由他们的国家奥委会报名；

4.5.1.1.2　遵守公平竞争和非暴力的竞赛原则，并在赛场上做出相应的表现；

4.5.1.1.3 遵守《世界反兴奋剂条例》并在所有方面遵照执行；

4.5.1.1.4 在奥运会期间，不得将他们的身份、姓名、照片或运动行为用于广告目的，除非得到国际奥委会执行委员会允许。

4.5.1.2 运动员报名或参与奥运会，不得以经济上的考虑为条件。

4.5.1.3 国家奥委会报名的运动员必须是该国国民。

4.5.1.3.1 如果一名运动员同时是两个或以上国家的国民，他（她）可以选择代表其中一个国家。

4.5.1.3.2 一名运动员在奥运会、洲际或地区运动会，或在国际乒联认可的世界或地区锦标赛中代表了一个国家参赛，该运动员就不能代表另一个国家参赛，除非他（她）符合 4.5.1.3.3 条款中所列的条件。

4.5.1.3.3 除规则 3.8 条款的规定外，获得新国籍并希望代表新协会的国家奥委会参加奥运会的运动员，应通过新协会向国际乒联注册。从国际乒联确认运动员注册之日起，或从运动员获得新国籍之日起，以较早者为准，视为已注册。

4.5.1.3.4 运动员在下列下情况下不得代表新的国家奥委会：

4.5.1.3.4.1 如果运动员注册时年龄未满 15 岁，自注册之日起未满 3 年，或者该运动员从未代表过其他协会，但自注册之日起未满 1 年；

4.5.1.3.4.2 如果运动员注册时年满 15 岁但未到 18 岁，自注册之日起未满 5 年；

4.5.1.3.4.3 如果运动员注册时年满 18 岁但未到 21 岁，自注册之日起未满 7 年；

4.5.1.3.4.4　如果运动员注册时已满 21 岁，自注册之日起未满 9 年。

4.5.1.3.5　如果一个联合州、省或海外地区、一个国家或殖民地获得独立，如果一个国家因为边界改变而与另一个国家合并，如果一个新的国家奥委会得到国际奥委会承认，那么运动员可以继续代表他（她）属于或曾属于的国家。但是，如果他（她）愿意，也可以选择代表新的国家，并由新的国家奥委会报名参加奥运会。这样的选择只能有一次。

4.5.1.4　已经参加过奥运会的运动员应保留其参赛资格。

4.5.1.5　所有关于一名运动员是否能在奥运会代表一个国家参赛的争议，特别是关于运动员的国籍、公民身份或居住地的具体要求，包括等待期的长短等问题，将由国际奥委会执行委员会做出决定。

4.5.2　竞赛项目

4.5.2.1　奥运会比赛至少包括男子单打、女子单打、男子团体和女子团体。

4.5.2.2　团体比赛的赛制，以及团体和单项比赛，包括所有预选赛的竞赛方法，应由董事会根据洲理事会的建议做出决定，并依照国际奥委会制定的日程安排通知所有协会。

4.5.2.3　来自同一协会的运动员，根据 3.6.3.1 和 3.6.3.3 条款规定，仅在预选赛的轮次合理分开，后续轮次不再考虑。

4.5.3　兴奋剂检测

4.5.3.1　兴奋剂检测将根据国际奥委会的规定及《世界反兴奋剂条例》执行。

4.6 残奥会比赛

4.6.1 资格

4.6.1.1 有资格参加残奥会的运动员、教练员或官员，应遵守《国际残疾人奥林匹克委员会章程》和国际乒联规则。以上人员还应该是：

4.6.1.1.1 由他们的国家残奥委会报名；

4.6.1.1.2 遵守公平竞争和非暴力的竞赛原则，并在赛场上做出相应的表现；

4.6.1.1.3 遵守《世界反兴奋剂条例》并在所有方面遵照执行；

4.6.1.1.4 在残奥会期间，不得将他们的身份、姓名、照片或运动行为用于广告目的，除非得到国际残奥委会理事会的允许。

4.6.1.2 运动员报名或参与残奥会，不得以经济上的考虑为条件。

4.6.1.3 国家残奥委会报名的运动员必须是该国国民。

4.6.1.3.1 如果一名运动员同时是两个或以上国家的国民，他（她）可以选择代表其中一个国家。

4.6.1.3.2 一名运动员在残奥会、洲际或地区运动会，或在国际乒联认可的世界或地区锦标赛中代表了一个国家参赛，该运动员就不能代表另一个国家参赛，除非他（她）符合4.6.1.3.3条款中所列的条件。

4.6.1.3.3 除规则3.8条款的规定外，获得新国籍并希望代表新协会的国家残奥会运动员，应通过新协会向国际乒联注册。从国际乒联确认运动员注册之日起，或从运动员获得新国籍之日起，以较早者为准，视为已注册。

4.6.1.3.4 运动员在下列情况下不得代表新的国家残奥委会：

4.6.1.3.4.1　如果运动员注册时年龄未满 15 岁，自注册之日起未满 3 年，或者该运动员从未代表过其他协会，但自注册之日起未满 1 年；

4.6.1.3.4.2　如果运动员注册时年满 15 岁但未到 18 岁，自注册之日起未满 5 年；

4.6.1.3.4.3　如果运动员注册时年满 18 岁但未到 21 岁，自注册之日起未满 7 年；

4.6.1.3.4.4　如果运动员注册时已满 21 岁，自注册之日起未满 9 年。

4.6.1.3.5　如果一个联合州、省或海外地区、一个国家或殖民地获得独立，如果一个国家因为边界改变而与另一个国家合并，如果一个新的国家残奥委会得到国际残奥委会承认，那么运动员可以继续代表他（她）属于或曾属于的国家。但是，如果他（她）愿意，也可以选择代表新的国家，并由新的国家残奥委会报名参加残奥会。这样的选择只能有一次。

4.6.1.4　已经参加过残奥会的运动员应保留其参赛资格。

4.6.1.5　所有关于一名运动员是否能在残奥会代表一个国家参赛的争议，特别是关于运动员的国籍、公民身份或居住地的具体要求，包括等待期的长短等问题，将由国际残奥委会理事会做出决定。

4.6.2　竞赛项目

4.6.2.1　残奥会比赛至少包括男子和女子分级别单打、男子和女子团体比赛，以及国际残奥委会理事会根据洲理事会的建议，纳入的任何其他项目。

4.6.2.2　团体比赛的赛制，以及团体和单项比赛，包括所有预选赛的竞赛方法，应由董事会根据洲理事会的建议做出决定，并依照国际残奥委会制定的日程安排通知所有协会。

4.6.3　兴奋剂检测

4.6.3.1　兴奋剂检测将根据国际残奥委会的规定及《世界反兴奋剂条例》执行。

4.7　世界残疾人乒乓球锦标赛

4.7.1　组织的权力

4.7.1.1　世界残疾人乒乓球锦标赛，本部分简称"残疾人乒乓球锦标赛"，为国际乒联执行委员会指定锦标赛设立项目并委托某协会承办的比赛。

4.7.1.2　申请举办残疾人乒乓球锦标赛截止日期由执行委员会确定，并至少在 6 个月前通知所有协会。

4.7.1.3　所有申请应与遴选委员会的报告一起送交执行委员会审核，如有可能，包括届时相关场馆的报告。

4.7.1.4　如有必要，执行委员会可以安排一个或几个相关的委员会成员去申办残疾人乒乓球锦标赛的协会考察，以确信申办方提出的比赛和其他安排是否适当，考察的费用由该协会承担。

4.7.1.5　主办协会确定下来后，如果情况发生变化并可能影响到残疾人乒乓球锦标赛的顺利举办时，执行委员会可以在比赛前撤销主办权。

4.7.2　主办协会的职责

4.7.2.1　协会一旦获准举办残疾人乒乓球锦标赛，就称为"主办协会"。主办协会应该根据《乒乓球规则》、《乒乓球国际竞赛规程》和《世界比赛规程》，以及经理事会修改和补充的竞赛指南组织比赛。

4.7.2.2　　主办协会应该从残疾人乒乓球锦标赛开始前一个晚上起，到比赛结束的第二天上午止，为下列人员提供食宿：

4.7.2.2.1　国际乒联执行委员会和残疾人乒乓球委员会成员；

4.7.2.2.2　根据国际乒联颁布的指南所邀请的其他协会的国际级裁判员和裁判长；

4.7.2.2.3　根据国际乒联颁布的指南所邀请的 5 名国际分级师；

4.7.2.2.4　国际乒联工作人员，最多 3 人。

4.7.2.3　　如果国际乒联的业务工作超过残疾人乒乓球锦标赛的时间，主办协会应相应延长对参加该业务的人员的食宿招待。

4.7.2.4　　主办协会应该对参赛者免费提供医疗和药品，但是每个协会必须为自己的运动员和官员在残疾人乒乓球锦标赛期间投保疾病和伤害险。

4.7.2.5　　主办协会应负担参赛者往返驻地与比赛场馆间的交通费用。

4.7.2.6　　主办协会应要求本国政府免收所有参赛者的签证费。

4.7.2.7　　主办协会应确保所有的运动员、官员以及 4.7.2.2 条款所列的人员可随意进出比赛场馆以及在相关的比赛区域活动。编外运动员、委员会成员以及国际乒联任命的翻译、医生或医疗顾问也同样享有这种待遇。

4.7.2.8　　主办协会至少应提供一流的英语翻译服务。

4.7.2.9　　主办协会应在场馆内为国际乒联提供办公室，并提供翻译、计算机、互联网、电话、传真和复印等设备供其使用。

4.7.2.10　主办协会应该发行一份比赛指南，详细介绍残疾人乒乒球锦标赛的组织情况，内容包括：

4.7.2.10.1　残疾人乒乓球锦标赛的日期和地点；

4.7.2.10.2　残疾人乒乓球锦标赛的项目；

4.7.2.10.3　残疾人乒乓球锦标赛使用的器材；

4.7.2.10.4　残疾人乒乓球锦标赛的报名程序、报名费以及所需承诺；

4.7.2.10.5　抽签的日期和地点；

4.7.2.10.6　仲裁会议的日期；

4.7.2.10.7　技术官员及国际乒联官员的接待范围；

4.7.2.10.8　在住宿、交通及场馆方面，针对残疾人的辅助设施；

4.7.2.10.9　运动员和官员的最大数量；

4.7.2.10.10　任何由理事会对该残疾人乒乓球锦标赛颁发的指令。

4.7.2.11　在残疾人乒乓球锦标赛期间，主办协会应及时为国际乒联执行委员会成员、残疾人乒乓球委员会成员和各队的领队提供包括详细比分的比赛成绩；比赛结束后，主办协会应尽快公布包括详细比分的整套成绩册，并分发给所有协会。

4.7.3　资格

4.7.3.1　只有未拖欠会费（1.7.3.3）的协会，才有资格在残疾人乒乓球锦标赛中为其运动队或运动员报名。

4.7.3.2　除规则 3.8 条款的规定外，获得新国籍并希望代表该国籍对应协会的运动员，应通过新协会向国际乒联注册。从国际乒联确认运动员注册之日起，或从运动员获得新国籍之日起，以较早者为准，视为已注册。

4.7.3.3　运动员在下列情况下不得代表新协会：

4.7.3.3.1　如果运动员注册时年龄未满 15 岁，自注册之日起未满

3 年，或者该运动员从未代表过其他协会，但自注册之日起未满 1 年；

4.7.3.3.2　如果运动员注册时年满 15 岁但未到 18 岁，自注册之日起未满 5 年；

4.7.3.3.3　如果运动员注册时年满 18 岁但未到 21 岁，自注册之日起未满 7 年；

4.7.3.3.4　如果运动员注册时已满 21 岁，自注册之日起未满 9 年。

4.7.3.4　已经参加过世界残疾人乒乓球锦标赛的运动员保留其参赛资格。

4.7.4　报名费

4.7.4.1　报名费由主办协会上报并经残疾人乒乓球委员会同意后确定。

4.7.4.2　参赛协会在报名时应该向主办协会交纳报名费，报名费包含由残疾人乒乓球委员会不定期设定的人头费。

4.7.4.3　因不可控制的原因而不能参加残疾人乒乓球锦标赛的协会，可不向理事会缴纳报名费，除此之外，每一个报名的协会都应按时交纳报名费。

4.7.5　递交报名表

4.7.5.1　报名的截止日期由主办协会在得到残疾人乒乓球委员会的批准后确定，但最晚不超过残疾人乒乓球锦标赛开始前 2 个月。

4.7.5.2　应提交有编号和姓名的报名表；报名表由主办协会随竞赛规程一同发布。

4.7.5.3　每个协会每个级别最多可以报 3 名运动员，每个国家每个级别可报 1 个团体。

4.7.5.4　协会应按技术水平为报名的运动员排序，排序应符合当时的世界排名。

4.7.5.5　国际乒联只接受有参赛资格协会的正式报名，报名表必须由协会的负责人签名，并在截止日期当日或之前被收到。

4.7.6　报名的更改

4.7.6.1　经技术代表的同意，协会可以更改报名。

4.7.6.2　根据首席分级师的建议，裁判长可以更改报名。

4.7.7　报名须知

4.7.7.1　报名表应包括一个由协会负责人代表、所有运动员及官员签署的声明，承诺团队的成员遵守国际乒联反兴奋剂条例及国际乒联分级准则，并表明他们理解和接受残疾人乒乓球锦标赛的条件，准备和所有的对手进行竞争，没有该声明，报名表无效。

4.7.7.2　单项比赛中，所有的参赛者都被视为个人选手；无论其他的参赛对手是否来自同一协会，运动员都应尽最大努力赢得所有参加的比赛，并且不能退出比赛，除非受伤或生病。

4.7.8　仲裁委员会

4.7.8.1　仲裁委员会由残疾人乒乓球委员会任命的 3 名代表组成。

4.7.8.2　任何受仲裁会议正在审议事项直接影响的协会，应有权派代表出席仲裁会议，但无权投票。

4.7.8.3　仲裁委员会有权对在竞赛管理委员会管辖范围内的申诉做出裁决，可批准团体和分级变动。

4.7.8.4　在残疾人乒乓球锦标赛开始以前，仲裁委员会就应召开仲裁会议，通报当时所有的抽签变更，仅当出现对行政和**分级决定**或裁判长的决定提出申诉时，仲裁委员会应再次召开仲裁会议。

4.7.9　竞赛项目

4.7.9.1　残疾人乒乓球锦标赛应至少包括男子和女子分级单打、男子和女子团体项目，以及残疾人乒乓球**委员会**纳入的任何其他项目。

4.7.9.2　各项目的比赛方法及实施日期应由残疾人乒乓球**委员会**根据技术专员的建议来决定。

4.7.10　兴奋剂检测

4.7.10.1　兴奋剂检测应按照国际乒联反兴奋剂条例执行。

4.7.11　奖励和仪式

4.7.11.1　团体和单项比赛，在决赛中获胜的运动员将获得金牌，在决赛中失利的运动员将获得银牌，在半决赛中获胜的运动员将获得铜牌。

4.7.11.2　团体和单项比赛的颁奖仪式，应悬挂金牌、银牌和铜牌获得者国家的国旗，奏金牌获得者国家的国歌。

4.7.12　商业权利

4.7.12.1　国际乒联在全球范围内独家享有和控制锦标赛及相关的所有商业权利，该商业权利包括但不限于以下所有方面：

4.7.12.1.1　音频、视频、音视频及数据版权（存于每种媒介，**无论在这些条款发布之日是否存在**）；

4.7.12.1.2　赞助、广告、销售、市场推广及其他形式的结社权；

4.7.12.1.3　票务、接待及其他特许经营权；

4.7.12.1.4　锦标赛商业化的其他权利（包括但不限于任何所谓"赛

事权"和任何授权对锦标赛进行投注的权利）。

4.7.12.2　国际乒联有权以其认为合适的方式开发其商业权利，包括不定期地给相关的协会或其他第三方发放同等（或部分）权利许可证。

4.7.12.3　每个协会应确保他们的成员（官员、运动员、代表和其他隶属机构）应：

4.7.12.3.1　完全遵守任何及所有的规则、规程，以及由国际乒联或其代表不定期颁布的与商业权利开发相关的指南；

4.7.12.3.2　提供所要求的权利、设施和服务以确保国际乒联和／或相关第三方得以在开发任何商业权利的合约下履行其义务，并且不得以任何作为或者不作为侵犯根据本协议授予的任何独家权利，或以其他方式造成违约。为避免疑义，只有国际乒联可针对某协会强制执行此规则，没有第三方有权这样做。

4.8　世界元老锦标赛

4.8.1　组织的权利

4.8.1.1　世界元老锦标赛，本部分简称"锦标赛"，由董事会指定锦标赛设立项目并委托某协会承办的比赛。

4.8.1.2　锦标赛可以由协会以外的有必要设施的其他机构（地区协会、俱乐部等）组织，但协会以外的组织必须得到其批准。该协会将成为国际乒联的合作伙伴。

4.8.1.3　申请锦标赛的截止日期由执行委员会确定，并至少在6个月前通知所有协会。

4.8.1.4　所有申请应与遴选委员会的报告一起送交执行委员会审核并提交给董事会，如有可能，应包括届时相关场馆的报告。

4.8.1.5　　如有必要，董事会或执行委员会可以安排一位或几位相关的委员会成员去申办锦标赛的协会考察，以确信申办方提出的比赛和其他安排是否适当，考察的费用由该协会承担。

4.8.1.6　　主办协会确定下来后，如果情况发生变化并可能影响到锦标赛的顺利举办时，则该举办权可以在锦标赛前的董事会会议上以多数表决的方式撤销；在董事会会议期间，执行委员会有权将锦标赛改在异地或采取任何其他适当的行动。

4.8.2　　主办协会的职责

4.8.2.1　　协会一旦获准举办锦标赛，就称为"主办协会"。主办协会应该根据《乒乓球规则》、《乒乓球国际竞赛规程》和《世界比赛规程》，以及由董事会修改和补充的竞赛指南组织比赛。

4.8.2.2　　2 名国际乒联竞赛部成员 2 次视察（通常在申办陈述后 6 个月内及比赛开始前 6 个月内）的费用（共计 4 人的差旅费及食宿费用）由主办协会承担。如有必要再次视察，将与主办协会商讨详情并达成一致。

4.8.2.3　　主办协会应当提供免费内部交通（驻地到比赛场馆，酒店到最近国际机场的抵离），和从锦标赛开始前一天中午起，到比赛结束后的第二天上午止，为以下人员提供食宿：

4.8.2.3.1　　由执行委员会在与元老委员会和斯韦思林俱乐部商议后提名的 10 名参赛者（最好是 5 男 5 女）；

4.8.2.3.2　　比赛开始前 5 天，组织比赛的 3 人（主要是电脑专家和国际乒联竞赛经理）；

4.8.2.3.3 比赛开始前 3 天，由斯韦思林俱乐部执行委员会提名的 7 人；

4.8.2.3.4 国际乒联执行委员会全体成员及国际乒联元老委员会主席；

4.8.2.3.5 根据国际乒联《关于世界锦标赛比赛官员的指导意见》邀请的其他协会的国际级裁判员和裁判长；

4.8.2.3.6 最多 4 名国际乒联工作人员。

4.8.2.4 如果国际乒联的业务超出了锦标赛比赛时间，参与该业务的人员的接待时间应相应地延长。

4.8.2.5 主办协会将在比赛场地为所有参赛者提供免费急救 / 医疗服务。所有参赛者对自己的身体和心理健康负责，并且必须持有锦标赛期间的疾病、事故和伤害的健康保险。

4.8.2.6 主办协会应在场馆内为国际乒联和斯韦思林俱乐部提供办公室，配备翻译、电脑、互联网、电话和复印等设备供其使用。

4.8.2.7 主办协会应该发行一份比赛指南，详细介绍锦标赛的组织情况，内容包括：

4.8.2.7.1 锦标赛的日期和地点；

4.8.2.7.2 锦标赛的类别和项目；

4.8.2.7.3 锦标赛使用的器材；

4.8.2.7.4 锦标赛的报名程序、报名费以及所需承诺；

4.8.2.7.5 抽签日期、地点；

4.8.2.7.6 仲裁会议和社交活动的日期；

4.8.2.7.7 技术官员的接待范围；

4.8.2.7.8　　任何董事会对锦标赛颁发的指令。

4.8.2.8　　　锦标赛期间，主办协会应及时、定时公开展示所有成绩，包括详细比分。

4.8.2.8.1　　锦标赛结束后，主办协会应立即向国际乒联提交各年龄组别奖牌获得者的最终排名，以及颁奖典礼上所有奖牌颁发给运动员的照片。

4.8.2.8.2　　所有成绩将公布在赛事官方网站和国际乒联官方网站。

4.8.3　　资格

4.8.3.1　　在锦标赛当年，年龄 40 岁以上或即将 40 岁的个人均有资格参赛。

4.8.3.2　　每位参赛者可参加一项单打和一项双打。在双打中，不一定参加自己的年龄组别，但总是在配对 2 人中较为年轻的组别。

4.8.4　　报名费

4.8.4.1　　报名费和随行人员费用由国际乒联执行委员会和主办协会共同决定。

4.8.4.2　　在 4.8.2.3.1 条款中列出的 10 名受邀参赛者将不收取报名费。

4.8.4.3　　报名费应在参赛时支付给主办协会。

4.8.5　　资格赛

4.8.5.1　　锦标赛分资格赛和正选比赛 2 个阶段举行。未取得正选参赛资格的选手，可选择参加安慰赛。

4.8.5.2　　资格赛在锦标赛第一天进行，采用分组循环。每组的第一名和第二名将有资格参加正选比赛。其余选手可以选择参加安慰赛。

4.8.5.3　　如果一个年龄组的参赛选手少于 6 人或 6 对，竞赛经理可以决定只用一组进行循环赛，确切的比赛办法将在比赛开始前公布。

4.8.5.4 正选比赛及安慰赛采用淘汰制。

4.8.6 报名须知

4.8.6.1 网上报名表包含要求参赛者承诺遵守国际乒联反兴奋剂条例，要求接受国际乒联球拍检测条例，并确认在锦标赛中能够与其他所有参赛者进行比赛的声明。

4.8.6.2 所有参赛者均作为个人参赛；无论其他参赛对手是否来自同一协会，参赛者都应尽最大努力赢得比赛，除疾病或受伤的原因，不得退出比赛。

4.8.6.3 一旦参赛，表明参赛者同意遵守国际乒联的所有比赛规则和规程。所有参赛运动员同意由国际乒联及其代理人主导所有有关电视转播、视频转播、网络直播、电影转播和任何形式的摄影转播事宜。参赛运动员放宽所有的，或其代理人或赞助商持有的所有有关电视转播、视频转播、网络直播、电影转播和任何形式的摄影转播事宜的权利。如参赛者拒绝上述转播事宜，将会被暂停或取消比赛资格。

4.8.7 仲裁委员会

4.8.7.1 仲裁委员会由 3 名代表组成：国际乒联元老委员会主席（担任仲裁主席）、1 名组委会代表、1 名国际乒联竞赛部代表。

4.8.7.2 裁判长或副裁判长将被邀请出席仲裁会议，有发言权但无投票权。

4.8.7.3 仲裁委员会有权对竞赛管理委员会管辖范围内的任何申诉问题做出裁决。

4.8.7.4 只能对裁判长的决定提出申诉，必须在该场比赛结束后立即以书面形式提出。

4.8.7.5 仲裁成员不得以运动员身份参加比赛。

4.8.8 竞赛项目

4.8.8.1 锦标赛至少包括男子单打、女子单打、男子双打和女子双打。

4.8.8.2 每项比赛的年龄分组为：

40 至 44 岁（+40 岁），

45 至 49 岁（+45 岁），

50 至 54 岁（+50 岁），

55 至 59 岁（+55 岁），

60 至 64 岁（+60 岁），

65 至 69 岁（+65 岁），

70 至 74 岁（+70 岁），

75 至 79 岁（+75 岁），

80 至 84 岁（+80 岁），

85 至 89 岁（+85 岁），

90 岁及以上（+90 岁）。

4.8.8.3 如果任何一项赛事的参赛者少于 4 人，竞赛经理有权取消该项目或为相关运动员引用合理的替代方案。任何改动 / 取消应尽快通知参赛者。

4.8.9 缺席

4.8.9.1 每个参赛者有义务按照赛程规定的球台和时间比赛。

4.8.9.2 每个参赛者有责任随时了解比赛的时间和地点。

4.8.10 兴奋剂检测

4.8.10.1 兴奋剂检测应按照国际乒联反兴奋剂条例执行。

4.8.11　　　奖励和仪式

4.8.11.1　　　所有项目中，在决赛中获胜的运动员将获得金牌，在决赛中失利的运动员将获得银牌，在半决赛中失利的运动员将获得铜牌。

4.8.11.2　　　如某年龄组只有一个小组的资格赛而没有正赛，则按该组的最终排名，颁发奖牌给该组排名第一、第二、第三名的选手或配对。

4.8.11.3　　　安慰赛的第一名和第二名将获得一份小纪念品和刻有其姓名的证书。

4.8.12　　　商业权利

4.8.12.1　　　国际乒联在全球范围内独家享有和控制锦标赛及相关的所有商业权利，该商业权利包括但不限于以下所有方面：

4.8.12.1.1　　音频、视频、音视频及数据版权（存于每种媒介，无论在这些条款发布之日是否存在）；

4.8.12.1.2　　赞助、广告、销售、市场推广及其他形式的结社权；

4.8.12.1.3　　票务、接待及其他特许经营权；

4.8.12.1.4　　锦标赛商业化的其他权利（包括但不限于任何所谓"赛事权"和任何授权对锦标赛进行投注的权利）。

4.8.12.2　　　国际乒联有权以其认为合适的方式开发其商业权利，包括不定期地给相关的协会或其他第三方发放同等（或部分）权利许可证。

4.8.12.3　　　所有锦标赛的参赛者（官员、运动员、代表和其他隶属机构）应：

4.8.12.3.1　　完全遵守任何及所有的规则、规程，以及由国际乒联或其代表不定期颁布的与商业权利开发相关的指南；

4.8.12.3.2　提供所要求的权利、设施和服务以确保国际乒联和 /
　　　　　或相关第三方得以在开发任何商业权利的合约下履行
　　　　　其义务，并且不得以任何作为或者不作为侵犯根据本
　　　　　协议授予的任何独家权利，或以其他方式造成违约。
　　　　　为避免疑义，只有国际乒联可针对某协会强制执行此
　　　　　规则，没有第三方有权这样做。

4.8.13　　　暂时条款

4.8.13.1　执行委员会将根据现有斯韦思林俱乐部的权利和义务
　　　　　批准 2022 年赛事指南，以维护 2022 年世界元老锦标
　　　　　赛主办协会的权利和义务。

附　录　2022年国际乒乓球联合会手册（英文相应部分）

1　　CONSTITUTION

（略）

2 THE LAWS OF TABLE TENNIS

2.1 THE TABLE

2.1.1 The upper surface of the table, known as the playing surface, shall be rectangular, 2.74m long and 1.525m wide, and shall lie in a horizontal plane 76cm above the floor.

2.1.2 The playing surface shall not include the vertical sides of the tabletop.

2.1.3 The playing surface may be of any material and shall yield a uniform bounce of about 23cm when a standard ball is dropped on to it from a height of 30cm.

2.1.4 The playing surface shall be uniformly dark coloured and matt, but with a white side line, 2cm wide, along each 2.74m edge and a white end line, 2cm wide, along each 1.525m edge.

2.1.5 The playing surface shall be divided into 2 equal courts by a vertical net running parallel with the end lines, and shall be continuous over the whole area of each court.

2.1.6 For doubles, each court shall be divided into 2 equal half-courts by a white centre line, 3mm wide, running parallel with the side lines; the centre line shall be regarded as part of each right half-court.

2.2 THE NET ASSEMBLY

2.2.1 The net assembly shall consist of the net, its suspension and the supporting posts, including the clamps attaching them to the table.

2.2.2 The net shall be suspended by a cord attached at each end to an upright post 15.25cm high, the outside limits of the post being 15.25cm outside the side line.

2.2.3 The top of the net, along its whole length, shall be 15.25cm above the playing surface.

2.2.4　The bottom of the net, along its whole length, shall be as close as possible to the playing surface and the ends of the net shall be attached to the supporting posts from top to bottom.

2.3　THE BALL

2.3.1　The ball shall be spherical, with a diameter of 40mm.

2.3.2　The ball shall weigh 2.7g.

2.3.3　The ball shall be made of celluloid or similar plastics material and shall be white or orange, and matt.

2.4　THE RACKET

2.4.1　The racket may be of any size, shape or weight but the blade shall be flat and rigid.

2.4.2　At least 85% of the blade by thickness shall be of natural wood; an adhesive layer within the blade may be reinforced with fibrous material such as carbon fibre, glass fibre or compressed paper, but shall not be thicker than 7.5% of the total thickness or 0.35mm, whichever is the smaller.

2.4.3　A side of the blade used for striking the ball shall be covered with either ordinary pimpled rubber, with pimples outwards having a total thickness including adhesive of not more than 2.0mm, or sandwich rubber, with pimples inwards or outwards, having a total thickness including adhesive of not more than 4.0mm.

2.4.3.1　Ordinary pimpled rubber is a single layer of non-cellular rubber, natural or synthetic, with pimples evenly distributed over its surface at a density of not less than 10 per cm² and not more than 30 per cm².

2.4.3.2　Sandwich rubber is a single layer of cellular rubber covered with a single outer layer of ordinary pimpled rubber, the thickness of the pimpled rubber not being more than 2.0mm.

2.4.4　The blade, any layer within the blade and any layer of covering material or adhesive on a side used for striking the ball shall be continuous and of even thickness. Material suitable to shape a handle for holding the racket may be added on.

2.4.5 The covering material shall extend up to but not beyond the limits of the blade, except that the part nearest the handle and gripped by the fingers may be left uncovered or covered with any material.

2.4.6 The surface of the covering material on a side of the blade, or of a side of the blade if it is left uncovered, shall be matt, black on one side, and of a bright colour clearly distinguishable from black and from the colour of the ball on the other.

2.4.7 The racket covering shall be used without any physical, chemical or other treatment.

2.4.7.1 Slight deviations from continuity of surface or uniformity of colour as well as helpful or protective fittings may be allowed provided that they do not significantly change the characteristics of the surface.

2.4.8 Before the start of a match and whenever he or she changes his or her racket during a match a player shall show his or her opponent and the umpire the racket he or she is about to use and shall allow them to examine it.

2.5 DEFINITIONS

2.5.1 A rally is the period during which the ball is in play.

2.5.2 The ball is in play from the last moment at which it is stationary on the palm of the free hand before being intentionally projected in service until the rally is decided as a let or a point.

2.5.3 A let is a rally of which the result is not scored.

2.5.4 A point is a rally of which the result is scored.

2.5.5 The racket hand is the hand carrying the racket.

2.5.6 The free hand is the hand not carrying the racket; the free arm is the arm of the free hand.

2.5.7 A player strikes the ball if he or she touches it in play with his or her racket, held in the hand, or with his or her racket hand below the wrist.

2.5.8 A player obstructs the ball if he or she, or anything he or she wears or carries, touches it in play when it is above or travelling towards the playing surface, not having touched his or her court since last being struck by his or her opponent.

2.5.9   The server is the player due to strike the ball first in a rally.

2.5.10   The receiver is the player due to strike the ball second in a rally.

2.5.11   The umpire is the person appointed to control a match.

2.5.12   The assistant umpire is the person appointed to assist the umpire with certain decisions.

2.5.13   Anything that a player wears or carries includes anything that he or she was wearing or carrying, other than the ball, at the start of the rally.

2.5.14   The end line shall be regarded as extending indefinitely in both directions.

2.6   THE SERVICE

2.6.1   Service shall start with the ball resting freely on the open palm of the server's stationary free hand.

2.6.2   The server shall then project the ball near vertically upwards, without imparting spin, so that it rises at least 16cm after leaving the palm of the free hand and then falls without touching anything before being struck.

2.6.3   As the ball is falling the server shall strike it so that it touches first his or her court and then touches directly the receiver's court; in doubles, the ball shall touch successively the right half court of server and receiver.

2.6.4   From the start of service until it is struck, the ball shall be above the level of the playing surface and behind the server's end line, and it shall not be hidden from the receiver by the server or his or her doubles partner or by anything they wear or carry.

2.6.5   As soon as the ball has been projected, the server's free arm and hand shall be removed from the space between the ball and the net. The space between the ball and the net is defined by the ball, the net and its indefinite upward extension.

2.6.6   It is the responsibility of the player to serve so that the umpire or the assistant umpire can be satisfied that he or she complies with the requirements of the Laws, and either may decide that a service is incorrect.

2.6.6.1　If either the umpire or the assistant umpire is not sure about the legality of a service he or she may, on the first occasion in a match, interrupt play and warn the server; but any subsequent service by that player or his or her doubles partner which is not clearly legal shall be considered incorrect.

2.6.7　Exceptionally, the umpire may relax the requirements for a correct service where he or she is satisfied that compliance is prevented by physical disability.

2.7　THE RETURN

2.7.1　The ball, having been served or returned, shall be struck so that it touches the opponent's court, either directly or after touching the net assembly.

2.8　THE ORDER OF PLAY

2.8.1　In singles, the server shall first make a service, the receiver shall then make a return and thereafter server and receiver alternately shall each make a return.

2.8.2　In doubles, except as provided in 2.8.3, the server shall first make a service, the receiver shall then make a return, the partner of the server shall then make a return, the partner of the receiver shall then make a return and thereafter each player in turn in that sequence shall make a return.

2.8.3　In doubles, when at least one player of a pair is in a wheelchair due to a physical disability, the server shall first make a service, the receiver shall then make a return but thereafter either player of the disabled pair may make returns.

2.9 A LET

2.9.1 The rally shall be a let:

2.9.1.1   if in service the ball touches the net assembly, provided the service is otherwise correct or the ball is obstructed by the receiver or his or her partner;

2.9.1.2   if the service is delivered when the receiving player or pair is not ready, provided that neither the receiver nor his or her partner attempts to strike the ball;

2.9.1.3   if failure to make a service or a return or otherwise to comply with the Laws is due to a disturbance outside the control of the player;

2.9.1.4   if play is interrupted by the umpire or assistant umpire;

2.9.1.5   if the receiver is in wheelchair owing to a physical disability and in service the ball, provided that the service is otherwise correct,

2.9.1.5.1   after touching the receiver's court returns in the direction of the net;

2.9.1.5.2   comes to rest on the receiver's court;

2.9.1.5.3   in singles leaves the receiver's court after touching it by either of its sidelines.

2.9.2 Play may be interrupted

2.9.2.1   to correct an error in the order of serving, receiving or ends;

2.9.2.2   to introduce the expedite system;

2.9.2.3   to warn or penalise a player or adviser;

2.9.2.4   because the conditions of play are disturbed in a way which could affect the outcome of the rally.

2.10 A POINT

2.10.1 Unless the rally is a let, a player shall score a point

2.10.1.1   if an opponent fails to make a correct service;

2.10.1.2   if an opponent fails to make a correct return;

2.10.1.3   if, after he or she has made a service or a return, the ball touches anything other than the net assembly before being struck by an opponent;

2.10.1.4　　if the ball passes over his or her court or beyond his or her end line without touching his or her court, after being struck by an opponent;

2.10.1.5　　if the ball, after being struck by an opponent, passes through the net or between the net and the net post or between the net and playing surface;

2.10.1.6　　if an opponent obstructs the ball;

2.10.1.7　　if an opponent deliberately strikes the ball more than once in succession;

2.10.1.8　　if an opponent strikes the ball with a side of the racket blade whose surface does not comply with the requirements of 2.4.3, 2.4.4 and 2.4.5;

2.10.1.9　　if an opponent, or anything an opponent wears or carries, moves the playing surface;

2.10.1.10　if an opponent, or anything an opponent wears or carries, touches the net assembly;

2.10.1.11　if an opponent's free hand touches the playing surface;

2.10.1.12　if a doubles opponent strikes the ball out of the sequence established by the first server and first receiver;

2.10.1.13　as provided under the expedite system (2.15.4).

2.10.1.14　if both players or pairs are in a wheelchair due to a physical disability and

2.10.1.14.1　his or her opponent does not maintain a minimum contact with the seat or cushion(s), with the back of the thigh, when the ball is struck;

2.10.1.14.2　his or her opponent touches the table with either hand before striking the ball;

2.10.1.14.3　his or her opponent's footrest or foot touches the floor during play.

2.10.1.15　if, where an opposing doubles pair includes at least one player in a wheelchair, any part of the wheelchair or a foot of a standing player crosses an imaginary extension of the centre line of the table.

2.11 A GAME

2.11.1 A game shall be won by the player or pair first scoring 11 points unless both players or pairs score 10 points, when the game shall be won by the first player or pair subsequently gaining a lead of 2 points.

2.12 A MATCH

2.12.1 A match shall consist of the best of any odd number of games.

2.13 THE ORDER OF SERVING, RECEIVING AND ENDS

2.13.1 The right to choose the initial order of serving, receiving and ends shall be decided by lot and the winner may choose to serve or to receive first or to start at a particular end.

2.13.2 When one player or pair has chosen to serve or to receive first or to start at a particular end, the other player or pair shall have the other choice.

2.13.3 After each 2 points have been scored the receiving player or pair shall become the serving player or pair and so on until the end of the game, unless both players or pairs score 10 points or the expedite system is in operation, when the sequences of serving and receiving shall be the same but each player shall serve for only 1 point in turn.

2.13.4 In each game of a doubles match, the pair having the right to serve first shall choose which of them will do so and in the first game of a match the receiving pair shall decide which of them will receive first; in subsequent games of the match, the first server having been chosen, the first receiver shall be the player who served to him or her in the preceding game.

2.13.5 In doubles, at each change of service the previous receiver shall become the server and the partner of the previous server shall become the receiver.

2.13.6 The player or pair serving first in a game shall receive first in the next game of the match and in the last possible game of a doubles match the pair due to receive next shall change their order of receiving when first one pair scores 5 points.

2.13.7　The player or pair starting at one end in a game shall start at the other end in the next game of the match and in the last possible game of a match the players or pairs shall change ends when first one player or pair scores 5 points.

2.14　OUT OF ORDER OF SERVING, RECEIVING OR ENDS

2.14.1　If a player serves or receives out of turn, play shall be interrupted by the umpire as soon as the error is discovered and shall resume with those players serving and receiving who should be server and receiver respectively at the score that has been reached, according to the sequence established at the beginning of the match and, in doubles, to the order of serving chosen by the pair having the right to serve first in the game during which the error is discovered.

2.14.2　If the players have not changed ends when they should have done so, play shall be interrupted by the umpire as soon as the error is discovered and shall resume with the players at the ends at which they should be at the score that has been reached, according to the sequence established at the beginning of the match.

2.14.3　In any circumstances, all points scored before the discovery of an error shall be reckoned.

2.15　THE EXPEDITE SYSTEM

2.15.1　Except as provided in 2.15.2, the expedite system shall come into operation after 10 minutes' play in a game or at any time when requested by both players or pairs.

2.15.2　The expedite system shall not be introduced in a game if at least 18 points have been scored.

2.15.3　If the ball is in play when the time limit is reached and the expedite system is due to come into operation, play shall be interrupted by the umpire and shall resume with service by the player who served in the rally that was interrupted; if the ball is not in play when the expedite system comes into operation, play shall resume with service by the player who received in the immediately preceding rally.

2.15.4　Thereafter, each player shall serve for 1 point in turn until the end of the game, and if the receiving player or pair makes 13 correct returns in a rally the receiver shall score a point.

2.15.5　Introduction of the expedite system shall not alter the order of serving and receiving in the match, as defined in 2.13.6.

2.15.6　Once introduced, the expedite system shall remain in operation until the end of the match.

3 REGULATIONS FOR INTERNATIONAL COMPETITIONS

3.1 SCOPE OF LAWS AND REGULATIONS

3.1.1 Types of Competition

3.1.1.1 An international competition is one that may include the players of more than one Association.

3.1.1.2 An international match is a match between teams representing Associations.

3.1.1.3 An open tournament is one that is open to the players of all Associations.

3.1.1.4 A restricted tournament is one that is restricted to specified groups of players other than age groups.

3.1.1.5 An invitation tournament is one that is restricted to specified Associations or players, individually invited.

3.1.2 Applicability

3.1.2.1 Except as provided in 3.1.2.2, the Laws (Chapter 2) shall apply to World, Continental, Olympic and Paralympic title competitions, open tournaments and, unless otherwise agreed by the participating Associations, to international matches.

3.1.2.2 The Executive Committee shall have power to authorise the organiser of an open tournament to adopt temporary law variations.

3.1.2.3 The Regulations for International Competitions shall apply to:

3.1.2.3.1 World, Olympic and Paralympic title competitions, unless otherwise authorised by the Board of Directors and notified in advance to the participating Associations;

3.1.2.3.2 Continental title competitions, unless otherwise authorised by the appropriate Continental Federation and notified in advance to the participating Associations;

3.1.2.3.3 Open International Championships (3.7.1.2), unless otherwise authorised by the Executive Committee and notified in advance to the participants in accordance with 3.1.2.4;

3.1.2.3.4 open tournaments, except as provided in 3.1.2.4.

3.1.2.4 Where an open tournament does not comply with any of these regulations the nature and extent of the variation shall be specified in the entry form; completion and submission of an entry form shall be regarded as signifying acceptance of the conditions of the competition, including such variations.

3.1.2.5 The Laws and Regulations are recommended for all international competitions but, provided that the Constitution is observed, international restricted and invitation tournaments and recognised international competitions organised by unaffiliated bodies may be held under rules laid down by the organising authority.

3.1.2.6 The Laws and the Regulations for International Competitions shall be presumed to apply unless variations have been agreed in advance or are made clear in the published rules of the competition.

3.1.2.7 Detailed explanations and interpretations of Rules, including equipment specifications for International Competitions, shall be published as Technical or Administrative Leaflets by the Board of Directors; practical instructions and implementation procedures may be issued as Handbooks or Guides by the Executive Committee. These publications may include mandatory parts as well as recommendations or guidance.

3.2 EQUIPMENT AND PLAYING CONDITIONS
3.2.1 Approved and Authorised Equipment

3.2.1.1 The approval and authorisation of playing equipment shall be conducted on behalf of the Board of Directors by the Equipment Committee; an approval or authorisation may be suspended by the Executive Committee at any time and subsequently the approval or authorisation may be withdrawn by the Board of Directors.

3.2.1.2　The entry form or prospectus for an open tournament shall specify the brands and colours of table, net assembly, flooring and ball to be used; the choice of table, net assembly and ball shall be as laid down by the ITTF or by the Association in whose territory the competition is held, selected from brands and types currently approved by the ITTF; for selected ITTF sanctioned tournaments, the flooring shall be of a brand and type currently approved by ITTF.

3.2.1.3　Any ordinary pimpled rubber or sandwich rubber covering the racket shall be currently authorised by the ITTF and shall be attached to the blade so that the ITTF logo, the ITTF number (when present), the supplier and brand names are clearly visible nearest the handle.

Lists of all approved and authorised equipment and materials are maintained by the ITTF Office and details are available on the ITTF website.

3.2.1.4　Table legs shall be at least 40cm from the end line of the table for wheelchair players.

3.2.2　Playing Clothing

3.2.2.1　Playing clothing shall consist of a short-sleeved or sleeveless shirt and shorts or skirt or one-part sports outfits, socks and playing shoes; other garments, such as part or all of a tracksuit, shall not be worn during play except with the permission of the referee.

3.2.2.2　The main colour of a shirt, skirt or shorts, other than sleeves and collar of a shirt shall be clearly different from that of the ball in use.

3.2.2.3　Clothing may bear numbers or lettering on the back of the shirt to identify a player, his or her Association or, in club matches, his or her club, and advertisements in accordance with the provisions of 3.2.5.9; if the back of a shirt bears the player's name, this shall be situated just below the collar.

3.2.2.4 Any numbers required by organisers to identify a player shall have priority over advertisements on the centre part of the back of a shirt; such numbers shall be contained within a panel having an area not greater than 600cm^2.

3.2.2.5 Any markings or trimming on the front or side of a playing garment and any objects such as jewellery worn by a player shall not be so conspicuous or brightly reflecting as to unsight an opponent.

3.2.2.6 Clothing shall not carry designs or lettering which might cause offence or bring the game into disrepute.

3.2.2.7 The players of a team taking part in a team match, and players of the same Association forming a doubles pair in a World, Olympic or Paralympic Title Competition, shall be dressed uniformly, with the possible exception of socks, shoes and the number, size, colour and design of advertisements on clothing.

3.2.2.8 Opposing players and pairs shall wear shirts that are of sufficiently different colours to enable them to be easily distinguished by spectators.

3.2.2.9 Where opposing players or teams have a similar shirt and cannot agree which of them will change, the decision shall be made by the umpire by lot.

3.2.2.10 Players competing in a World, Olympic or Paralympic title competition shall wear shirt and shorts or skirt of types authorised by their Association.

3.2.3 Playing Conditions

3.2.3.1 The playing space shall be rectangular and not less than 14m long, 7m wide and 5m high, but the 4 corners may be covered by surrounds of not more than 1.5m length; for wheelchair events, the playing space may be reduced, but shall not be less than 8m long and 6m wide; for Veteran events, the playing space may be reduced, but shall not be less than 10m long and 5m wide.

3.2.3.2 The following equipment and fittings are to be considered as part of each playing area: The table including the net assembly, printed numbers identifying the table, flooring, umpires tables and chairs, score indicators, towel and ball boxes, surrounds, boards on the surrounds indicating the names of players or Associations, and small technical equipment which shall be fitted in a way that does not affect play.

3.2.3.3　　The playing area shall be enclosed by surrounds about 75cm high, all of the same dark background colour, separating it from adjacent playing areas and from spectators.

3.2.3.4　　In World, Olympic and Paralympic title competitions the light intensity, measured at the height of the playing surface, shall be at least 1500 lux uniformly over the whole of the playing surface and at least 1000 lux elsewhere in the playing area; in other competitions the intensity shall be at least 1000 lux uniformly over the playing surface and at least 600 lux elsewhere in the playing area.

3.2.3.5　　Where several tables are in use, the lighting level shall be the same for all of them, and the level of background lighting in the playing hall shall not be greater than the lowest level in the playing area.

3.2.3.6　　The light source shall not be less than 5m above the floor.

3.2.3.7　　The background shall be generally dark and shall not contain bright light sources or daylight through uncovered windows or other apertures.

3.2.3.8　　The flooring shall not be light-coloured, brightly reflecting or slippery and it shall be resilient; the flooring may be rigid for wheelchair events.

3.2.3.8.1　　In World, Olympic and Paralympic title competitions the flooring shall be of wood or of a brand and type of rollable synthetic material authorised by the ITTF.

3.2.3.9　　Technical equipment on the net assembly shall be considered part of it.

3.2.4 Racket Control

3.2.4.1   It is the responsibility of each player to ensure that racket coverings are attached to their racket blade with adhesives that do not contain harmful volatile solvents.

3.2.4.2   A racket control centre shall be established at all ITTF World Title, Olympic and Paralympic competitions as well as at a select number of other ITTF competitions and may be established at Continental and Regional competitions.

3.2.4.2.1   The racket control centre shall test rackets, according to the policy and procedure established by the Executive Committee on recommendation of the Equipment Committee and Umpires and Referees Committee, to ensure that rackets abide by all ITTF regulations including, but not limited to, flatness, racket covering thickness, even thickness and continuity of layers, and presence of harmful or volatile substances.

3.2.4.2.2   Normally, the racket control test shall be carried out before the match. After-match tests shall only be conducted, where the racket was not submitted on time for a before-match test or for tests or inspections that could not be performed before the match.

3.2.4.2.3   Rackets that do not pass the racket control test before the match cannot be used but may be replaced by a second racket which may be tested immediately if time permits, but if not, will be tested after the match; in the case where rackets do not pass a random racket control test after the match, the offending player will be liable to penalties.

3.2.4.2.4   All players are entitled to have their rackets tested voluntarily without any penalties before the match.

3.2.4.3   Following 4 accumulated failures on any aspect of racket testing in a period of four years, the player may complete the event, but subsequently the Executive Committee will suspend the offending player for 12 months.

3.2.4.3.1   The ITTF shall inform the suspended player in writing of such suspension.

3.2.4.3.2　The suspended player may appeal to the ITTF Tribunal within 21 days of the receiving of the letter of suspension; should such an appeal be submitted, the player's suspension would remain in force.

3.2.4.4　The ITTF shall maintain a register of all racket control failures with effect from 1 September 2010.

3.2.4.5　A properly ventilated area shall be provided for the attachment of racket coverings to rackets, and liquid adhesives shall not be used anywhere else at the playing venue.

"Playing venue" means that part of the building used for table tennis and its related activities, facilities and public area.

3.2.5　Advertisements and Markings

3.2.5.1　Inside the playing area, advertisements shall be displayed only on equipment or fittings listed in 3.2.3.2 or on playing clothing, umpires' clothing or players' numbers and there shall be no special additional displays.

3.2.5.1.1　Advertisements or markings in or next to the playing area, on playing clothing or numbers and on umpires' clothing, shall not be for tobacco goods, alcoholic drinks, harmful drugs or illegal products and they shall be without negative discrimination or connotation on the grounds of race, xenophobia, gender, religion, disabilities or other forms of discrimination; however, for competitions not explicitly organised for players under 18 years of age, the ITTF may allow advertisements or markings for non-distilled alcoholic drinks on equipment and fittings in or next to the playing area, provided the local law permits.

3.2.5.2　At Olympic and Paralympic Games advertisements on playing equipment, on playing clothing and on umpires' clothing shall be according to IOC and IPC regulations respectively.

3.2.5.3　With the exception of LED (light-emitting diode) and similar devices advertisements on the surrounds of the sides of the playing area, fluorescent, luminescent or glossy colours shall not be used anywhere in the playing area and the background colour of the surrounds shall remain dark.

3.2.5.3.1　　Advertisements on surrounds shall not change during a match from dark to light and vice versa.

3.2.5.3.2　　LEDs and similar devices on surrounds shall not be so bright as to disturb players during the match and shall not change when the ball is in play.

3.2.5.3.3　　Advertisements on LED and similar devices shall not be used without prior approval from ITTF.

3.2.5.4　　Lettering or symbols on the inside of surrounds shall be clearly different from the colour of the ball in use, not more than two colours and shall be contained within a height of 40cm.

3.2.5.5　　There may be up to 6 advertisements on the floor of the playing area; such markings

3.2.5.5.1　　may be placed 2 at each end, each contained within an area of 5m^2, and 1 at each side of the table, each contained within an area of 2.5m^2;

3.2.5.5.2　　at the end shall not be less than 3m from the table's end line next to the marking;

3.2.5.5.3　　shall be of the same uniform colour different from the colour of the ball in use, unless other colours have been agreed in advance with the ITTF;

3.2.5.5.4　　shall not alter significantly the surface friction of the flooring;

3.2.5.5.5　　shall consist only of a logo, wordmark or other icons, and shall not include any background.

3.2.5.6　　Advertisements on the table shall comply with the following requirements:

3.2.5.6.1　　There may be 1 permanent advertisement of the manufacturer's or supplier's name or logo on each half of each side of the table top and on each end.

3.2.5.6.2　　There may be 1 temporary advertisement, which also can be of the manufacturer's or supplier's name or logo, on each half of each side of the table top and on each end.

3.2.5.6.3   Each permanent and each temporary advertisement shall be contained within a total length of 60cm.

3.2.5.6.4   Temporary advertisements shall be clearly separated from any permanent advertisements.

3.2.5.6.5   Advertisements shall not be for other table tennis equipment suppliers.

3.2.5.6.6   There shall be no advertisement, name of table, name or logo of the manufacturer or supplier of the table on the undercarriage, except if the table manufacturer or supplier is the title sponsor of the tournament.

3.2.5.7   There may be 2 temporary advertisements on nets on each side of the table which shall be clearly different from the colour of the ball in use, shall not be within 3cm of the tape along the top edge; advertisements placed on parts of the net within the vertical extensions of the side lines of the table shall be a logo, wordmark or other icons.

3.2.5.8   Advertisements on umpires' tables or other furniture inside the playing area shall be contained within a total area on any face of $750cm^2$.

3.2.5.9   Advertisements on playing clothing shall be limited to

3.2.5.9.1   the maker's normal trademark, symbol or name contained within a total area of $24cm^2$;

3.2.5.9.2   not more than 6 clearly separated advertisements, contained within a combined total area of $600cm^2$, on the front, side or shoulder of a shirt, with not more than 4 advertisements on the front;

3.2.5.9.3   not more than 2 advertisements, contained within a total area of $400cm^2$, on the back of a shirt;

3.2.5.9.4   not more than 2 advertisements, contained within a combined total area of $120cm^2$, only on the front and the sides of shorts or skirt.

3.2.5.10   Advertisements on players' numbers shall be contained within a total area of 100cm^2; if such numbers are not used there may be additional temporary advertisements for tournament sponsors within a total area of 100 cm^2.

3.2.5.11 Advertisements on umpires' clothing shall be contained within a total area of 40cm^2.

3.2.6 Doping Control

3.2.6.1 All players participating in international competitions, including Junior competitions, shall be subject to in-competition testing by the ITTF, the player's Member Association and any other Anti-Doping Organisation responsible for testing at a competition in which they participate.

3.2.7 Table Tennis Review

3.2.7.1 An electronic table tennis review system (TTR) may be used, and it will come into effect when an appeal is made by a player against a decision of a responsible match official on a question of fact. TTR will provide a replay of the circumstances leading to a decision subject to a review, with the final decision to the appeal made by a TTR official.

3.3 MATCH OFFICIALS

3.3.1 Referee

3.3.1.1 For each competition as a whole a referee shall be appointed and his or her identity and location shall be made known to the participants and, where appropriate, to the team captains.

3.3.1.2 The referee shall be responsible for:

3.3.1.2.1 the conduct of the draw;

3.3.1.2.2 the scheduling of the matches by time and table;

3.3.1.2.3 the appointment of match officials;

3.3.1.2.4 conducting a pre-tournament briefing for match officials;

3.3.1.2.5 checking the eligibility of players;

3.3.1.2.6 deciding whether play may be suspended in an emergency;

3.3.1.2.7   deciding whether players may leave the playing area during a match;

3.3.1.2.8   deciding whether statutory practice periods may be extended;

3.3.1.2.9   deciding whether players may wear track suits during a match;

3.3.1.2.10   deciding any question of interpretation of Laws or Regulations, including the acceptability of clothing, playing equipment and playing conditions;

3.3.1.2.11   deciding whether, and where, players may practise during an emergency suspension of play;

3.3.1.2.12   taking disciplinary action for misbehaviour or other breaches of regulations.

3.3.1.3   Where, with the agreement of the competition management committee, any of the duties of the referee are delegated to other persons, the specific responsibilities and locations of each of these persons shall be made known to the participants and, where appropriate, to the team captains.

3.3.1.4   The referee, or a responsible deputy appointed to exercise authority in his or her absence, shall be present at all times during play.

3.3.1.5   Where the referee is satisfied that it is necessary to do so he or she may replace a match official with another at any time, but he or she may not alter a decision already made by the replaced official on a question of fact within his or her jurisdiction.

3.3.1.6   Players shall be under the jurisdiction of the referee from the time at which they arrive at the playing venue until they leave it.

3.3   Umpire, Assistant Umpire, Stroke Counter and Table Tennis Review (TTR) Official

3.3.2.1   An umpire and an assistant umpire shall be appointed for each match.

3.3.2.2   The umpire shall sit or stand in line with the net and the assistant umpire shall sit directly facing him or her, at the other side of the table.

3.3.2.3   The umpire shall be responsible for:

3.3.2.3.1   checking the acceptability of equipment and playing conditions and reporting any deficiency to the referee;

3.3.2.3.2   taking a ball at random as provided in 3.4.2.1.1-2;

3.3.2.3.3   conducting the draw for the choice of serving, receiving and ends;

3.3.2.3.4   deciding whether the requirements of the service law may be relaxed for a player with physical disability;

3.3.2.3.5   controlling the order of serving, receiving and ends and correcting any errors therein;

3.3.2.3.6   deciding each rally as a point or a let;

3.3.2.3.7   calling the score, in accordance with specified procedure;

3.3.2.3.8   introducing the expedite system at the appropriate time;

3.3.2.3.9   maintaining the continuity of play;

3.3.2.3.10   taking action for breaches of the advice or behaviour regulations;

3.3.2.3.11   drawing by lot which player, pair or team shall change their shirt, should opposing players or teams have a similar shirt and cannot agree which of them will change.

3.3.2.3.12   ensuring that only authorised persons are at the playing area.

3.3.2.4   The assistant umpire shall:

3.3.2.4.1   decide whether or not the ball in play touches the edge of the playing surface at the side of the table nearest him or her;

3.3.2.4.2   inform the umpire for breaches of the advice or behaviour regulations.

3.3.2.5   Either the umpire or the assistant umpire may:

3.3.2.5.1   decide that a player's service action is illegal;

3.3.2.5.2   decide that, in an otherwise correct service, the ball touches the net assembly;

3.3.2.5.3   decide that a player obstructs the ball;

3.3.2.5.4   decide that the conditions of play are disturbed in a way that may affect the outcome of the rally;

3.3.2.5.5   time the duration of the practice period, of play and of intervals.

3.3.2.6　　Either the assistant umpire or a separate official may act as stroke counter, to count the strokes of the receiving player or pair when the expedite system is in operation.

3.3.2.7　　A decision made by the assistant umpire in accordance with the provisions of 3.3.2.5 may not be overruled by the umpire.

3.3.2.8　　When Table Tennis Review (TTR) is in operation, a decision made by either the umpire or assistant umpire may be overruled by the TTR official.

3.3.2.9　　Players shall be under the jurisdiction of the umpire from the time at which they arrive at the playing area until they leave it.

3.3 Appeals

3.3.3.1　　No agreement between players, in an individual event, or between team captains, in a team event, can alter a decision on a question of fact by the responsible match official, on a question of interpretation of Laws or Regulations by the responsible referee or on any other question of tournament or match conduct by the responsible management committee.

3.3.3.2　　No appeal may be made to the referee against a decision on a question of fact by the responsible match official or to the management committee on a question of interpretation of Laws or Regulations by the referee.

3.3.3.3　　When Table Tennis Review (TTR) is in operation, an appeal may be made to the TTR official against a decision of a responsible match official on a question of fact, and the decision of the TTR official shall be final.

3.3.3.4　　An appeal may be made to the referee against a decision of a match official on a question of interpretation of Laws or Regulations, and the decision of the referee shall be final.

3.3.3.5　　An appeal may be made to the competition management committee against a decision of the referee on a question of tournament or match conduct not covered by the Laws or Regulations, and the decision of the management committee shall be final.

3.3.3.6   In an individual event an appeal may be made only by a player participating in the match in which the question has arisen; in a team event an appeal may be made only by the captain of a team participating in the match in which the question has arisen.

3.3.3.7   A question of interpretation of Laws or Regulations arising from the decision of a referee, or a question of tournament or match conduct arising from the decision of a competition management committee, may be submitted by the player or team captain eligible to make an appeal, through his or her parent Association, for consideration by the ITTF Rules Committee.

3.3.3.8   The Rules Committee shall give a ruling as a guide for future decisions, and this ruling may also be made the subject of a protest by an Association to the Board of Directors or a General Meeting, but it shall not affect the finality of any decision already made by the responsible referee or management committee.

3.4   MATCH CONDUCT

3.4.1   Score Indication

3.4.1.1   The umpire shall call the score as soon as the ball is out of play at the completion of a rally, or as soon as is practicable thereafter.

3.4.1.1.1   In calling the score during a game the umpire shall call first the number of points scored by the player or pair due to serve in the next rally of the game and then the number of points scored by the opposing player or pair.

3.4.1.1.2   At the beginning of a game and when a change of server is due, the umpire shall point to the next server, and may also follow the score call with the next server's name.

3.4.1.1.3   At the end of a game the umpire shall call the number of points scored by the winning player or pair followed by the number of points scored by the losing player or pair and may then name the winning player or pair.

3.4.1.2   In addition to calling the score the umpire may use hand signals to indicate his or her decisions.

3.4.1.2.1   When a point has been scored, he or she may raise his or her arm nearer to the player or pair who won the point so that the upper arm is horizontal and the forearm is vertical with the closed hand upward.

3.4.1.2.2   When for any reason the rally is a let, he or she may raise his or her hand above his or her head to show that the rally has ended.

3.4.1.3   The score and, under the expedite system, the number of strokes shall be called in English or in any other language acceptable to both players or pairs and to the umpire.

3.4.1.4   The score shall be displayed on mechanical or electronic indicators so that it is clearly visible to the players and the spectators.

3.4.1.5   When a player is formally warned for bad behaviour, a yellow marker shall be placed on or near the score indicator.

3.4.2   Equipment

3.4.2.1   Players shall not choose balls in the playing area.

3.4.2.1.1   Wherever possible players shall be given the opportunity to choose one or more balls before coming to the playing area and the match shall be played with the ball chosen by the players.

3.4.2.1.2   If a ball has not been chosen before players come to the playing area, or the players cannot agree on the ball to be used, the match shall be played with a ball taken at random by the umpire from a box of those specified for the competition.

3.4.2.1.3   If a ball is damaged during a match, it shall be replaced by another of those chosen before the match or, if such a ball is not available, by one taken at random by the umpire from a box of those specified for the competition.

3.4.2.2   The racket covering shall be used as it has been authorised by the ITTF without any physical, chemical or other treatment, changing or modifying playing properties, friction, outlook, colour, structure, surface, etc.; in particular, no additives shall be used.

3.4.2.3　A racket shall successfully pass all parameters of the racket control tests.

3.4.2.4　A racket shall not be replaced during an individual match unless it is accidentally damaged so badly that it cannot be used; if this happens the damaged racket shall be replaced immediately by another which the player has brought with him or her to the playing area or one which is handed to him or her in the playing area.

3.4.2.5　Unless otherwise authorised by the umpire, players shall leave their rackets on the table during intervals; but if the racket is strapped to the hand, the umpire shall allow the player to retain his or her racket strapped to the hand during intervals.

3.4.3　Practice

3.4.3.1　Players are entitled to practise on the match table for up to 2 minutes immediately before the start of a match but not during normal intervals; the specified practice period may be extended only with the permission of the referee.

3.4.3.2　During an emergency suspension of play the referee may allow players to practise on any table, including the match table.

3.4.3.3　Players shall be given reasonable opportunity to check and to familiarise themselves with any equipment which they are to use, but this shall not automatically entitle them to more than a few practice rallies before resuming play after the replacement of a damaged ball or racket.

3.4.4　Intervals

3.4.4.1　Play shall be continuous throughout an individual match except that any player is entitled to:

3.4.4.1.1　an interval of up to 1 minute between successive games of an individual match;

3.4.4.1.2	brief intervals for towelling after every 6 points from the start of each game and at the change of ends in the last possible game of an individual match.
3.4.4.2	A player or pair may claim one time-out period of up to 1 minute during an individual match.
3.4.4.2.1	In an individual event the request for a time-out may be made by the player or pair or by the designated adviser; in a team event it may be made by the player or pair or by the team captain.
3.4.4.2.2	If a player or pair and an adviser or captain disagree whether a time-out is to be taken, the final decision shall be made by the player or pair in an individual event and by the captain in a team event.
3.4.4.2.3	The request for a time-out, which can be made only between rallies in a game, shall be indicated by making a "T" sign with the hands.
3.4.4.2.4	On receiving a valid request for a time-out the umpire shall suspend play and shall hold up a white card with the hand on the side of the player or pair who requested it; the white card or another appropriate marker shall be placed on the court of that player or pair.
3.4.4.2.5	The white card or marker shall be removed and play resumed as soon as the player or pair making the request is ready to continue or at the end of 1 minute, whichever is the sooner.
3.4.4.2.6	If a valid request for a time-out is made simultaneously by or on behalf of both players or pairs, play will resume when both players or pairs are ready or at the end of 1 minute, whichever is the sooner, and neither player or pair shall be entitled to another time-out during that individual match.
3.4.4.3	There shall be no intervals between successive individual matches of a team match except that a player who is required to play in successive matches may claim an interval of up to 5 minutes between those matches.

3.4.4.4　The referee may allow a suspension of play, of the shortest practical duration, and in no circumstances more than 10 minutes, if a player is temporarily incapacitated by an accident, provided that in the opinion of the referee the suspension is not likely to be unduly disadvantageous to the opposing player or pair.

3.4.4.5　A suspension shall not be allowed for a disability which was present or was reasonably to be expected at the beginning of the match, or where it is due to the normal stress of play; disability such as cramp or exhaustion, caused by the player's current state of fitness or by the manner in which play has proceeded, does not justify such an emergency suspension, which may be allowed only for incapacity resulting from an accident, such as injury caused by a fall.

3.4.4.6　If anyone in the playing area is bleeding, play shall be suspended immediately and shall not resume until that person has received medical treatment and all traces of blood have been removed from the playing area.

3.4.4.7　Players shall remain in or near the playing area throughout an individual match, except with the permission of the referee; during intervals between games and time-outs they shall remain within 3 metres of the playing area, under the supervision of the umpire.

3.5　DISCIPLINE

3.5.1　Advice

3.5.1.1　In a team event, players may receive advice from anyone authorised to be at the playing area.

3.5.1.2　In an individual event, a player or pair may receive advice only from one person, designated beforehand to the umpire, except that where the players of a doubles pair are from different Associations each may designate an adviser, but with regard to 3.5.1 and 3.5.2 these two advisers shall be treated as a unit; if an unauthorised person gives advice the umpire shall hold up a red card and send him or her away from the playing area.

3.5.1.3　Players may receive advice at any time except during rallies provided play is not thereby delayed (3.4.4.1); if any authorised person gives advice illegally the umpire shall hold up a yellow card to warn him or her that any further such offence will result in his or her dismissal from the playing area.

3.5.1.4　After a warning has been given, if in the same team match or the same match of an individual event anyone again gives advice illegally, the umpire shall hold up a red card and send him or her away from the playing area, whether or not he or she was the person warned.

3.5.1.5　In a team match the dismissed adviser shall not be allowed to return, except when required to play, and he or she shall not be replaced by another adviser until the team match has ended; in an individual event he or she shall not be allowed to return until the individual match has ended.

3.5.1.6　If the dismissed adviser refuses to leave, or returns before the end of the match, the umpire shall suspend play and report to the referee.

3.5.1.7　These regulations shall apply only to advice on play and shall not prevent a player or captain, as appropriate, from making a legitimate appeal nor hinder a consultation with an interpreter or Association representative on the explanation of a juridical decision.

3.5.2　Misbehaviour

3.5.2.1　Players and coaches or other advisers shall refrain from behaviour that may unfairly affect an opponent, offend spectators or bring the sport into disrepute, such as abusive language, deliberately breaking the ball or hitting it out of the playing area, kicking the table or surrounds and disrespect of match officials.

3.5.2.2　If at any time a player, a coach or another adviser commits a serious offence the umpire shall suspend play and report immediately to the referee; for less serious offences the umpire may, on the first occasion, hold up a yellow card and warn the offender that any further offence is liable to incur penalties.

3.5.2.3 Except as provided in 3.5.2.2 and 3.5.2.5, if a player who has been warned commits a second offence in the same individual match or team match, the umpire shall award 1 point to the offender's opponent and for a further offence he or she shall award 2 points, each time holding up a yellow and a red card together.

3.5.2.4 If a player against whom 3 penalty points have been awarded in the same individual match or team match continues to misbehave, the umpire shall suspend play and report immediately to the referee.

3.5.2.5 If a player changes his or her racket during an individual match when it has not been damaged, the umpire shall suspend play and report to the referee.

3.5.2.6 A warning or penalty incurred by either player of a doubles pair shall apply to the pair, but not to the non-offending player in a subsequent individual match of the same team match; at the start of a doubles match the pair shall be regarded as having incurred the higher of any warnings or penalties incurred by either player in the same team match.

3.5.2.7 Except as provided in 3.5.2.2, if a coach or another adviser who has been warned commits a further offence in the same individual match or team match, the umpire shall hold up a red card and send him or her away from the playing area until the end of the team match or, in an individual event, of the individual match.

3.5.2.8 The referee shall have power to disqualify a player from a match, an event or a competition for seriously unfair or offensive behaviour, whether reported by the umpire or not; as he or she does so he or she shall hold up a red card; for less serious offenses which do not justify disqualification, the referee may decide to report such an offense to the ITTF Integrity Unit.

3.5.2.9 If a player is disqualified from 2 matches of a team or individual event he or she shall automatically be disqualified from that team event or individual competition.

3.5.2.10 The referee may disqualify for the remainder of a competition anyone who has twice been sent away from the playing area during that competition.

3.5.2.11 If a player is disqualified from an event or competition for any reason, he or she shall automatically forfeit any associated title, medal, prize money or ranking points.

3.5.2.12 Cases of very serious misbehaviour shall be reported to the offender's Association.

3.5.2.13 The ITTF Integrity Unit may take further action for any serious, repeated or continuous violation of any provision under Article 3.5.2 and seek an imposition of one or more sanctions pursuant to the ITTF Integrity Regulations or the ITTF Tribunal Regulations.

3.5.3 Good Presentation

3.5.3.1 Players, coaches and officials shall uphold the object of good presentation of the sport and safeguard its integrity by refraining from any attempt to influence the elements of a competition in a manner contrary to sporting ethics:

3.5.3.1.1 Players have to do their utmost to win a match and shall not withdraw except for reasons of illness or injury.

3.5.3.1.2 Players, coaches and officials shall not participate in any form of or support betting or gambling related to their own matches and competitions.

3.5.3.2 Any player who deliberately fails to comply with these principles shall be disciplined by total or partial loss of prize money in prize events and/or by suspension from ITTF events.

3.5.3.3 In the event of complicity proven against any adviser or official the relevant Member Association is also expected to discipline this person.

3.5.3.4 The ITTF Integrity Unit may take further action for any serious, repeated or continuous violation of any provision under Article 3.5.3

and seek an imposition of one or more sanctions pursuant to the ITTF Integrity Regulations or the ITTF Tribunal Regulations.

3.6 DRAW FOR KNOCKOUT COMPETITIONS

3.6.1 Byes and Qualifiers

3.6.1.1 The number of places in the first-round proper of a knockout event shall be a power of 2.

3.6.1.1.1 If there are fewer entries than places, the first round shall include enough byes to make up the required number.

3.6.1.1.2 If there are more entries than places, a qualifying competition shall be held such that the number of qualifiers and the number of direct entries together make up the required number.

3.6.1.2 Byes shall be distributed as evenly as possible throughout the first round, being placed first against seeded places, in seeding order.

3.6.1.3 Qualifiers shall be drawn as evenly as possible among the halves, quarters, eighths or sixteenths of the draw, as appropriate.

3.6.2 Seeding by Ranking

3.6.2.1 The highest ranked entries in an event shall be seeded so that they cannot meet before the closing rounds.

3.6.2.2 The number of entries to be seeded shall not exceed the number of entries in the 1st round proper of the event.

3.6.2.3 The entry ranked 1 shall be placed at the top of the first half of the draw and the entry ranked 2 at the bottom of the second half, but all other seeded entries shall be drawn among specified places in the draw, as follows:

3.6.2.3.1 the entries ranked 3 and 4 shall be drawn between the bottom of the first half of the draw and the top of the second half;

3.6.2.3.2 the entries ranked 5-8 shall be drawn among the bottom places of the odd-numbered quarters of the draw and the top places of the even- numbered quarters;

3.6.2.3.3 the entries ranked 9-16 shall be drawn among the bottom places of the odd-numbered eighths of the draw and the top places of the even- numbered eighths;

3.6.2.3.4   the entries ranked 17-32 shall be drawn among the bottom places of the odd-numbered sixteenths of the draw and the top places of the even- numbered sixteenths.

3.6.2.4   In a team knockout event only the highest ranked team from an Association shall be eligible for seeding by ranking.

3.6.2.5   Seeding by ranking shall follow the order of the latest ranking list published by the ITTF except that:

3.6.2.5.1   where all the entries eligible for seeding are from Associations belonging to the same Continental Federation the latest list published by that Federation shall take precedence;

3.6.2.5.2   where all the entries eligible for seeding are from the same Association the latest list published by that Association shall take precedence.

3.6.3   Seeding by Association Nomination

3.6.3.1   Nominated players and pairs of the same Association shall, as far as possible, be separated according to 3.6.3.3 and 3.6.3.4 unless otherwise stated in the specific regulations for such particular event or group of events.

3.6.3.2   Associations shall list their nominated players and pairs in descending order of playing strength, starting with any players included in the ranking list used for seeding, in the order of that list.

3.6.3.3   The entries ranked 1 and 2 shall be drawn into different halves and those ranked 3 and 4 into quarters other than those occupied by the first two.

3.6.3.4   Remaining entries shall be separated only in groups and in the first round of the qualification draw for knockouts and the main draw, but not in further rounds.

3.6.3.5   A men's or women's doubles pair consisting of players from different Associations shall be considered a pair of the Association of the player ranked higher in the World Ranking List, or, if neither player is in this list, in the appropriate Continental Ranking List; if neither player is included in a World or Continental Ranking List, the pair shall be considered a member of the Association whose team is ranked higher in the appropriate World Team Ranking List.

3.6.3.6   A mixed doubles pair consisting of players from different Associations shall be considered a pair of the Association to which the man belongs.

3.6.3.7   Alternatively, any doubles pair consisting of players from different Associations may be considered a pair of both of these Associations.

3.6.3.8   In a qualifying competition, entries from the same Association, up to the number of qualifying groups, shall be drawn into separate groups in such a way that qualifiers are, as far as possible, separated in accordance with the principles of 3.6.3.3-4.

3.6.4   Alterations

3.6.4.1   A completed draw may be altered only with the permission of the responsible management committee and, where appropriate, the agreement of the representatives of Associations directly concerned.

3.6.4.2   The draw may be altered only to correct errors and genuine misunderstandings in the notification and acceptance of entry, to correct serious imbalance, as provided in 3.6.5, or to include additional players or pairs, as provided in 3.6.6.

3.6.4.3   No alterations other than necessary deletions shall be made to the draw of an event after it has started; for the purpose of this regulation a qualifying competition may be regarded as a separate event.

3.6.4.4   A player shall not be deleted from the draw without his or her permission, unless he or she is disqualified; such permission must be given either by the player if he or she is present or, if he or she is absent, by his or her authorised representative.

3.6.4.5   A doubles pair shall not be altered if both players are present and fit to play, but injury, illness or absence of one player may be accepted as justification for an alteration.

3.6.5　Re-draw

3.6.5.1　Except as provided in 3.6.4.2, 3.6.4.5 and 3.6.5.2, a player shall not be moved from one place in the draw to another and if for any reason the draw becomes seriously unbalanced the event shall, wherever possible, be completely re-drawn.

3.6.5.2　Exceptionally, where the imbalance is due to the absence of several seeded players or pairs from the same section of the draw, the remaining seeded players or pairs only may be re-numbered in ranking order and re-drawn to the extent possible among the seeded places, taking account as far as is practicable of the requirements for seeding by Association nomination.

3.6.6　Additions

3.6.6.1　Players not included in the original draw may be added later, at the discretion of the responsible management committee and with the agreement of the referee.

3.6.6.2　Any vacancies in seeded places shall first be filled, in ranking order, by drawing into them the strongest new players or pairs; any further players or pairs shall be drawn into vacancies due to absence or disqualification and then into byes other than those against seeded players or pairs.

3.6.6.3　Any players or pairs who would have been seeded by ranking if they had been included in the original draw may be drawn only into vacancies in seeded places.

3.7　ORGANISATION OF COMPETITIONS

3.7.1　Authority

3.7.1.1　Provided the Constitution is observed, any Association may organise or authorise open, restricted or invitation tournaments within its territory or may arrange international matches.

3.7.1.2   Except for Veteran events, players from affiliated ITTF member Associations, when competing internationally, can only participate in ITTF events, ITTF approved events and ITTF registered events entered through their Member Association, as well as in ITTF recognised events entered through their National Olympic Committee or National Paralympic Committee respectively. Participation in any other type of event can only be allowed with the express written permission of the Member Association of the player or the ITTF; permission to players will be considered given unless a specific or general notification is made by the national Association of the player or the ITTF withholding the permission to participate in an event or series of events.

3.7.1.3   A player or team may not take part in an international competition if he or she or it is suspended by his or her or its Association or Continental Federation.

3.7.1.4   No event may use a World title without the permission of the ITTF, or a Continental title without the permission of the appropriate Continental Federation.

3.7.2   Representation

3.7.2.1   Representatives of all Associations whose players are taking part in an Open International Championships event shall be entitled to attend the draw and shall be consulted on any alterations to the draw or any decisions of appeal that may directly affect their players.

3.7.3   Entries

3.7.3.1   Entry forms for Open International Championships shall be sent to all Associations not later than 2 calendar months before the start of the competition and not later than 1 calendar month before the date for the close of entries.

3.7.3.2　All entries nominated by Associations for open tournaments shall be accepted but the organisers shall have power to allocate entries to a qualifying competition; in deciding this allocation they shall take account of the relevant ITTF and Continental ranking lists and of any ranking order of entries specified by the nominating Association.

3.7.4　Events

3.7.4.1　Open International Championships shall include men's singles, women's singles, men's doubles and women's doubles and may include mixed doubles and international team events for teams representing Associations.

3.7.4.2　In world title competitions, players in youth events shall be under 19 and under 15 in age on 31st December immediately before the calendar year in which the competition takes place. The following age limits are recommended for corresponding events in other youth competitions: U21, U19, U17, U15, U13, U11.

3.7.4.3　It is recommended that team matches at Open International Championships be played according to one of the systems specified in 3.7.6; the entry form or prospectus shall show which system has been chosen.

3.7.4.4　Individual events proper shall be played on a knockout basis, but team events and qualifying rounds of individual events may be played on either a knockout or a group basis.

3.7.5　Group Competitions

3.7.5.1　In a group, or "round robin", competition, all members of the group shall compete against each other and shall gain 2 match points for a win, 1 for a loss in a played match and 0 for a loss in an unplayed or unfinished match; the ranking order shall be determined primarily by the number of match points gained. If a player is defaulted after the completion of a match for any reason, he or she shall be deemed to have lost the match, which shall subsequently be recorded as a loss in an unplayed match.

3.7.5.2　If two or more members of the group have gained the same number of match points their relative positions shall be determined only by the results of the matches between them, by considering successively the numbers of match points, the ratios of wins to losses first in individual matches (for a team event), games and points, as far as is necessary to resolve the order.

3.7.5.3　If at any step in the calculations the positions of one or more members of the group have been determined while the others are still equal, the results of matches in which those members took part shall be excluded from any further calculations needed to resolve the equalities in accordance with the procedure of 3.7.5.1 and 3.7.5.2.

3.7.5.4　If it is not possible to resolve equalities by means of the procedure specified in 3.7.5.1-3 the relative positions shall be decided by lot.

3.7.5.5　Unless otherwise authorised by the Jury, if 1 player or team is to qualify the final match in the group shall be between the players or teams numbered 1 and 2, if 2 are to qualify the final match shall be between the players or teams numbered 2 and 3 and so on.

3.7.6　Team Match Systems

3.7.6.1　Best of 5 matches (New Swaythling Cup system, 5 singles)

3.7.6.1.1　A team shall consist of 3 players.

3.7.6.1.2　The order of play shall be
1)A v X
2)B v Y
3)C v Z
4)A v Y
5)B v X

3.7.6.2　Best of 5 matches (Corbillon Cup system, 4 singles and 1 doubles)

3.7.6.2.1　A team shall consist of 2, 3 or 4 players.

3.7.6.2.2　The order of play shall be

    1)A v X
    2)B v Y
    3)doubles
    4)A v Y
    5)B v X

3.7.6.2.3   In Para TT events, the order of play may be as in 3.7.6.2.2 except that the doubles match may be played last.

3.7.6.3   Best of 5 matches (Olympic system, 4 singles and 1 doubles)

3.7.6.3.1   A team shall consist of 3 players; each player shall compete in a maximum of 2 individual matches.

3.7.6.3.2   The order of play shall be
    1)doubles B & C v Y & Z
    2)A v X
    3)C v Z
    4)A v Y
    5)B v X

3.7.6.4   Best of 7 matches (6 singles and 1 doubles)

3.7.6.4.1   A team shall consist of 3, 4 or 5 players.

3.7.6.4.2   The order of play shall be
    1)A v X
    2)B v Y
    3)C v Z
    4)doubles
    5)A v Y
    6)C v X
    7)B v Z

3.7.6.5   Best of 9 matches (9 singles)

3.7.6.5.1   A team shall consist of 3 players.

3.7.6.5.2   The order of play shall be
    1)A v X
    2)B v Y
    3)C v Z
    4)B v X

5)A v Z
6)C v Y
7)B v Z
8)C v X
9)A v Y

3.7.7 Team Match Procedure

3.7.7.1   All players shall be selected from those nominated for the event.

3.7.7.2   The name of the team captain, playing or non-playing, shall be designated beforehand to the umpire.

3.7.7.3   Before a team match the right to choose A, B, C or X, Y, Z shall be decided by lot and the captains shall name their teams to the referee or his or her representative, assigning a letter to each singles player.

3.7.7.4   The pairs for a doubles match need not be nominated until the end of the immediately preceding singles match.

3.7.7.5   A team match shall end when one team has won a majority of the possible individual matches.

3.7.8 Results

3.7.8.1   As soon as possible after the end of a competition and not later than 7 days thereafter the organising Association shall send to the ITTF Secretariat and to the Secretary of the appropriate Continental Federation details of the results, including points scores, of international matches, of all rounds of Continental and Open International Championships and of the closing rounds of national championships.

3.7.9 Television and Streaming

3.7.9.1   An event other than World, Continental, Olympic or Paralympic title competitions may be broadcast by television only with the permission of the Association from whose territory the broadcast is made.

3.7.9.2   Participation in an international event presumes the consent of the Association controlling the visiting players to the televising of that event; in World, Continental, Olympic or Paralympic title competitions such consent is presumed for the showing anywhere of live or recorded television during the period of the event and within 1 calendar month afterwards.

3.7.9.3   All streaming of ITTF events (all categories) shall be subject to compliance with the ITTF streaming certification process and a Streaming Certification Fee (SCF) shall be charged to the rights holder of the event.

3.8   INTERNATIONAL ELIGIBILITY

3.8.1   Eligibility in Olympic title competitions is regulated separately by 4.5.1 and eligibility in Paralympic title competitions is regulated separately by the IPC and 4.6.1; additional eligibility regulations apply to World title events (4.1.3, 4.2.3, 4.3.6, 4.4.3).

3.8.2   A player shall be regarded as representing an Association if he or she accepted to be nominated by this Association and subsequently participates in a competition listed in 3.1.2.3 or in regional championships other than individual events at Open International Championships.

3.8.3   A player is eligible to represent an Association only if he or she is a national of the country in which that Association has jurisdiction, except that a player who has already represented an Association of which he or she was not a national in accordance with previous rules may retain that eligibility.

3.8.3.1   Where the players of more than one Association have the same nationality, a player may represent one of these Associations only, if he or she is born in or has his or her main residence in the territory controlled by that Association.

3.8.3.2   A player who is eligible to represent more than 1 Association shall have the right to choose which of the relevant Associations he or she will represent.

3.8.4 A player is eligible to represent a Continental Federation (1.3.1) in an event of continental teams only if he or she is eligible to represent a member Association of this Continental Federation according to 3.8.3.

3.8.5 A player shall not represent different Associations within a period of 3 years.

3.8.6 An Association may nominate a player under its jurisdiction (1.8.4) to enter any individual events of Open International Championships; such nomination may be indicated in results lists and ITTF publications but does not affect the eligibility of this player according to 3.8.2.

3.8.7 A player or his or her Association shall, if so requested by the referee, provide documentary evidence of his or her eligibility and his or her passport.

3.8.8 Any appeal on a question of eligibility shall be referred to an Eligibility Commission, consisting of the Executive Committee, the Chair of the Rules Committee and the Chair of the Athletes' Commission, whose decision shall be final.

4　REGULATIONS FOR WORLD, OLYMPIC AND PARALYMPIC TITLE COMPETITIONS

4.1　WORLD CHAMPIONSHIPS

4.1.1　Authority for Organisation

4.1.1.1　The title "World Championships", referred to in this Section as "Championships", shall be bestowed by the AGM on the championship events at a tournament organised by an Association entrusted with the task.

4.1.1.2　The closing date for applications to stage Championships shall be specified by the Executive Committee and notified to all Associations, giving at least 6 months' notice.

4.1.1.3　All applications shall be considered by the Executive Committee and shall be submitted to the AGM, together with the report of the Selection Committee, if applicable, on venues for the occasion in question.

4.1.1.4　Where necessary, the AGM or the Executive Committee may ask one or more members of the appropriate Committee to visit the country of an Association applying for the right to organise the Championships to satisfy themselves as to the adequacy of the proposed playing and other arrangements; the cost of such visits shall be borne by that Association.

4.1.1.5　If, after an option has been granted, circumstances change in such a way as to be likely to prejudice the satisfactory conduct of the Championships, the option may be revoked by a 2/3 majority vote at an AGM prior to the Championships; between AGMs the Board of Directors shall have power to transfer the Championships or to take any other appropriate action.

4.1.2　Responsibilities of Organisers

4.1.2.1　An Association granted the right to organise the Championships, hereafter referred to as the "organisers" shall be responsible for conducting them in accordance with the Laws of Table Tennis, the Regulations for International Competitions and the Regulations for World Title Competitions, as modified or supplemented by any directives authorised by the Board of Directors.

4.1.2.2　Organisers shall provide accommodation and meals from lunch on the day before the Championships begin until breakfast on the day after the Championships end for:

4.1.2.2.1　not more than 2 men and 2 women players nominated by an Association;

4.1.2.2.2　1 delegate to the AGM from each Association if he is not already included in the nominated players listed above;

4.1.2.2.3　members of the Executive Committee, the Board of Directors and the Continental Council, full members of committees and the Technical and Gender Commissioners;

4.1.2.2.4　up to 3 Doping Control Supervisors appointed by the Sports Science and Medical Committee;

4.1.2.2.5　members of the Athletes' Commission not already included in the nominated players' lists;

4.1.2.2.6　Honorary Presidents;

4.1.2.2.7　Personal Honorary Members;

4.1.2.2.8　members of the President's Advisory Council;

4.1.2.2.9　International Umpires, Referees and Evaluators from other Associations invited in accordance with the ITTF directives for match officials at World Title Competitions;

4.1.2.2.10　up to 7 members of the ITTF staff including 1 assisting the Doping Control Supervisors.

4.1.2.3　If the business of the ITTF extends outside the period of the Championships the period of hospitality for those entitled to participate in such business shall be extended correspondingly.

4.1.2.4　Organisers shall provide free medical care and medicine for all participants, but each Association is recommended to insure its players and officials against illness and injury for the duration of the Championships.

4.1.2.5 Organisers shall meet the cost of transport between the place of accommodation and the playing hall.

4.1.2.6 Organisers shall request their national authorities to waive visa charges for all participants.

4.1.2.7 Organisers shall ensure free access to the playing hall and free circulation therein for all the players, officials and members listed in 4.1.2.2, for any additional players and committee members and for any interpreter, doctor or medical adviser appointed by the ITTF.

4.1.2.8 Organisers shall provide first-class interpreting in at least four languages, preferably by simultaneous translation with the appropriate equipment.

4.1.2.9 Organisers shall provide the ITTF with offices at the venue of the Championships and place at its disposal translation, computer, internet, telephone, telefax and duplicating facilities.

4.1.2.10 Organisers shall publish a prospectus giving the main details of the organisation of the Championships, including:

4.1.2.10.1 the dates and place of the Championships;

4.1.2.10.2 the events to be held;

4.1.2.10.3 the equipment to be used;

4.1.2.10.4 the procedure for entry, the entry fees and the undertakings required;

4.1.2.10.5 the date and place of the draw;

4.1.2.10.6 the dates of Jury meetings and of AGM sessions;

4.1.2.10.7 the extent of hospitality for players and officials;

4.1.2.10.8 any directives authorised by the Board of Directors for the Championships.

4.1.2.11 During the Championships Organisers shall make available promptly to members of the ITTF Executive Committee, Board of Directors members and team captain's details of results, including points scores; as soon as possible after the completion of the Championships Organisers shall publish the complete results, including points scores, and circulate them to all Associations.

4.1.3 Eligibility

4.1.3.1 Only an Association which is not in arrears (1.7.3.3) and has taken part with at least one player or team (an entry) in its preceding Continental Championships, including qualification tournaments, or Continental Games, shall be eligible to enter teams or individual players in the Championships.

4.1.3.2 In addition to provisions of 3.8, players who have acquired a new nationality and wish to represent the association corresponding to the new nationality shall register with ITTF through this new Association. A player is considered as registered either from the date of ITTF player registration confirmation or from the date the player is granted his or her new nationality, whichever is earlier.

4.1.3.3 Such player shall not represent the new Association before:

4.1.3.3.1 3 years after the date of registration, if the player is under the age of 15 when registered, but only 1 year after the date of registration if the player has never represented another association;

4.1.3.3.2 5 years after the date of registration, if the player is under the age of 18 but at least 15 years of age when registered;

4.1.3.3.3 7 years after the date of registration, if the player is under the age of 21 but at least 18 years of age when registered.

4.1.3.3.4 9 years after the date of registration, if the player is at least 21 years old when registered.

4.1.3.4 A player having participated already in World Championships shall retain his or her eligibility.

4.1.4 Entry Fees and Levy

4.1.4.1 The entry fees shall be US$100 for each entry in a team event, US$50 for each pair in a doubles event and US$25 for each entry in a singles event.

4.1.4.2　The entry fees shall be paid to the organisers at the time of entry and shall be shared equally between the organisers and the ITTF.

4.1.4.3　Fees for entries from an Association are due from that Association and shall always be payable, except that the Board of Directors may waive the fees where an Association is prevented from participating in the Championships by circumstances outside its control.

4.1.5　Submission of Entries

4.1.5.1　The intention to enter teams or players shall be notified to the ITTF in a preliminary notification form provided by the Secretariat; the closing date for the receipt of this form shall be not later than 4 calendar months before the start of the Championships.

4.1.5.2　Information shall be distributed, together with the prospectus, by the Competition Department and entries shall be submitted as required.

4.1.5.3　The closing date for the final entries shall be not later than 2 calendar months before the start of the Championships.

4.1.5.4　An Association may nominate up to 5 players and a non-playing captain for a team event; if a non-playing captain is not appointed one of the team players shall be designated as captain.

4.1.5.5　An Association shall rank its nominated players and pairs in order of playing strength, which shall be consistent with their current world ranking.

4.1.5.6　The ITTF may accept only formal nominations by an eligible Association, which are received, properly signed by a responsible representative of the nominating Association, on or before the closing date.

4.1.6　Modification of Entries

4.1.6.1　Modified entries shall be accepted, if notified by a representative of the nominating Association, at any time up to the day before the first official draw at World Championships (for individual events).

4.1.6.2   Change the composition of a team may be accepted if notified by a representative of the nominating Association up to the time of the Jury meeting preceding the World Team Championships; no further changes will be accepted after this deadline.

4.1.6.3   As soon as he or she arrives at the Championships venue, the representative of an Association requesting a change to the draw in consequence of any error or absence shall notify the referee or his or her deputy, or confirm any change already notified, on a form provided for the purpose.

4.1.6.4   A request for modification of an entry cannot be considered unless it is made or confirmed by the representative of an Association immediately on arrival, other than a request based on the subsequent absence, illness or injury of one player of a doubles pair, which shall be made as soon as the contingency arises.

4.1.6.5   All alterations that are authorised shall be notified immediately to team captains and, where appropriate, to Association representatives.

4.1.7   Entry Obligations

4.1.7.1   The entry form shall contain a statement, to be signed by a responsible representative of the nominating Association on behalf of all its nominated players and captains, that they understand and accept the conditions of the Championships and that they are prepared to compete against all other teams and individuals participating; no entry shall be valid unless accompanied by this declaration.

4.1.7.2   In individual events all entrants are accepted as individual competitors; they shall be bound to do their utmost to win the events for which they are entered, irrespective of whether other entrants from the same Association have been accepted to take part, and they shall not withdraw except for reasons of illness or injury.

4.1.8　Jury

4.1.8.1　The Jury shall consist of the Technical Commissioner, Chairs of the Technical, Rules and the Umpires' and Referees' Committees, a representative of the Competition Department, a representative of the organising committee and the referee; the referee shall have the right to speak but not to vote.

4.1.8.2　If any of the nominated Chairs is unable to attend a meeting of the Jury he or she may nominate to attend in his or her place another member of his or her Committee, who shall have the right to speak and to vote.

4.1.8.3　The Chair of the Jury shall be appointed by the members of the Jury.

4.1.8.4　Any Association directly affected by a matter under consideration at a Jury meeting shall be entitled to be represented at that meeting but shall not be entitled to vote.

4.1.8.5　The Jury shall have power to decide any question of appeal within the jurisdiction of a tournament management committee and to authorise team changes.

4.1.8.6　The Jury shall meet before the start of the Championships to be informed of all draw alterations requested up to that time and to decide any requests for changes in the composition of teams; any subsequent questions of draw alteration shall be decided by the Technical Commissioner in conjunction with a representative of the Competition Department and the Jury shall meet again only when convened by the Chair to consider appeals against its administrative decisions or decisions of the referee.

4.1.9　Events

4.1.9.1　In even numbered years, the Championships shall include men's team and women's team events; while in odd numbered years the Championships shall include men's singles, women's singles, men's doubles, women's doubles and mixed doubles events.

4.1.9.2　In doubles events, both players may be from different

Associations.

4.1.9.3 The system of play in team and individual events, the system of qualification in the team event and their implementation dates shall be decided by the Board of Directors, on the recommendation of the Technical Commissioner and the Competition Program.

4.1.9.4 Team matches shall be the best of 5 singles, as provided in 3.7.6.1.

4.1.9.5 There shall not be more than 128 places in the first round proper of a singles and not more than 64 places in the first round proper of a men's, women's and mixed doubles event, unless otherwise authorised by the Executive Committee.

4.1.9.6 Each Association shall be entitled to enter 3 men and 3 women players in each singles event, with one additional player ranked in the top 100 and one additional player ranked in the top 20 of the ITTF world ranking list issued in January of the year of the Championships to a maximum of 5 men and 5 women. The maximum entry for each association is 4 players for men's doubles, 4 players for women's doubles and 2 men and 2 women for mixed doubles; all players may be different, however, each association can only enter a maximum of 2 combined pairs (players from different associations) per doubles event.

4.1.9.6.1 The host Association may enter up to 6 men and 6 women in each singles event, 3 men's doubles, 3 women's doubles and 3 mixed doubles regardless of ranking.

4.1.9.7 Players of the same Association shall be separated according to 3.6.3.1, only in preliminary rounds and groups and in the first round of the draw but not in further rounds.

4.1.10 Default

4.1.10.1 An Association whose team is entered in the draw but which fails to compete in the event without adequate justification may be subject to disciplinary action by the AGM.

4.1.10.2 A team may begin, continue and complete a team match only with the full complement of players specified for the event, except that the referee may, at his or her discretion, allow a team to play with one player absent or an individual match to be omitted from the sequence where he or she is satisfied that the absence is due to accident, illness, injury or other circumstances outside the control of the player or the Association concerned, including disqualification by the referee in accordance with his or her authority.

4.1.10.3　An Association whose team begins to play in the event but which fails to complete its schedule of matches shall be liable to forfeit its entitlement to hospitality for its representatives at the Championships; an appeal against forfeit may be made to the Jury, whose decision shall be final.

4.1.11　Doping Control

4.1.11.1　Doping control shall be carried out in accordance with ITTF Anti-Doping rules (Chapter 5).

4.1.12　Awards and Presentations

4.1.12.1　The permanent Championship trophies shall be:

4.1.12.1.1　the Swaythling Cup for the men's team event;

4.1.12.1.2　the Marcel Corbillon Cup for the women's team event;

4.1.12.1.3　the St Bride Vase for the men's singles event;

4.1.12.1.4　the G Geist Prize for the women's singles event;

4.1.12.1.5　the Iran Cup for the men's doubles event;

4.1.12.1.6　the W J Pope Trophy for the women's doubles event;

4.1.12.1.7　the Heydusek prize for the mixed doubles event.

4.1.12.2　The Association whose team wins a team event, and the winner of an individual event, shall be entitled to hold the appropriate trophy until 31st December in the year following that in which it is won; the pair winning a doubles event shall agree or decide by lot the order in which each of them shall hold the trophy for half of the specified period.

4.1.12.3　A player who wins the men's or women's singles event 3 times in succession or 4 times in all shall receive from the ITTF a half-size replica of the appropriate trophy as a permanent possession.

4.1.12.4 In both team and individual events the winners shall receive gold medals, the losing finalists silver medals and the losing semi-finalists bronze medals.

4.1.12.5 At presentation ceremonies for both team and individual events the national flags of the gold, silver and bronze medal winners shall be raised and the national anthem of the gold medal winner shall be played.

4.1.12.6 The Association whose team or player wins a trophy shall acknowledge its receipt in writing and at the end of the specified period shall deliver it, within 14 days of a formal notification by the Secretariat, at an agreed time and to an agreed place.

4.1.12.7 The Association acknowledging receipt of a trophy shall be responsible for its safe keeping including the arrangement of insurance. The cost of insurance and of inscription of winners' names, which in team events should include any non-playing captain, shall be borne by the Association whose team or players wins a trophy.

4.1.12.8 If a trophy is lost while in the possession of an Association, that Association shall be responsible for the provision of a similar replacement.

4.1.12.9 At the closing ceremony the Egypt Cup, the symbol of the friendship of the Championships, shall be handed over to a representative of the city in which the next Championships will take place; this city shall hold the Egypt Cup until the next Championships.

4.1.13 Commercial Rights

4.1.13.1 The ITTF exclusively owns and controls all commercial rights in and to the Championships. Such Commercial Rights to include, without limitation and in each case on a worldwide basis, all:

4.1.13.1.1 audio, visual and audio-visual and data rights (in every medium, whether or not existing as at the date of these regulations);

4.1.13.1.2　　sponsorship, advertising, merchandising, marketing and other forms of rights of association;

4.1.13.1.3　　ticketing, hospitality and other concession rights; and

4.1.13.1.4　　other rights to commercialise the Championships (including without limitation any so-called "event rights" and any right to authorise the taking of bets on the Championships.

4.1.13.2　　The ITTF shall be entitled to exploit the Commercial Rights in such manner as it considers appropriate, including granting licences in respect of the same (or part thereof) to the relevant Association or to other third party(ies) from time to time.

4.1.13.3　　Each Association shall ensure that their members (officials, players, delegates and other affiliates) shall:

4.1.13.3.1　　comply with any and all rules, regulations and/or guidelines in relation to the exploitation of the Commercial Rights which may be issued from time to time by or on behalf of the ITTF; and

4.1.13.3.2　　provide such rights, facilities and services as are required to enable the ITTF and/or the relevant third party to fulfil their obligations under any arrangements for the exploitation of any of the Commercial Rights and shall not by any act or omission infringe any exclusive rights granted there under or otherwise cause any breach thereof to occur. For the avoidance of doubt only the ITTF may enforce this rule against an Association and no third party shall be entitled to do so.

4.2　　WORLD YOUTH CHAMPIONSHIPS

4.2.1　　Authority for Organisation

4.2.1.1　　The title "World Youth Championships", referred to in this Section as "Championships", shall be bestowed by the Board of Directors (Board) AGM on the championship events at a tournament organised by an Association entrusted with the task.

4.2.1.2 The closing date for applications to stage Championships shall be specified by the Executive Committee and notified to all Associations, giving at least 6 months' notice; applications shall be accepted only for the next 2 Championships.

4.2.1.3 All applications shall be considered by the Executive Committee and shall be submitted to the Board, together with details on venues for the occasion in question.

4.2.1.4 Where necessary, the Board or the Executive Committee may ask the Junior Commissioner to visit the country of an Association applying for the right to organise the Championships to satisfy themselves as to the adequacy of the proposed playing and other arrangements; the cost of such visits shall be borne by that Association.

4.2.1.5 If, after an option has been granted, circumstances change in such a way as to be likely to prejudice the satisfactory conduct of the Championships, the option may be revoked by a 2/3 majority vote at the AGM preceding the Championships; between AGMs the Board of Directors shall have power to transfer the Championships or to take any other appropriate action.

4.2.2 Responsibilities of Organisers

4.2.2.1 An Association granted the right to organise the Championships, hereafter referred to as the "organisers" shall be responsible for conducting them in accordance with the Laws of Table Tennis, the Regulations for International Competitions and the Regulations for World Youth Championships, as modified or supplemented by any directives authorised by the Board of Directors.

4.2.2.2 Organisers shall provide accommodation and meals from lunch on the day before the Championships begin until breakfast on the day after the Championships end for

4.2.2.2.1 not more than 2 boys players nominated by an Association eligible for the boys team event;

4.2.2.2.2 not more than 2 girls players nominated by an Association eligible for the girls team event;

4.2.2.2.3 not more than 1 coach of an Association participating in 1 or 2 team events;

4.2.2.2.4 members of the ITTF Executive Committee and the Junior Commissioner;

4.2.2.2.5 up to 2 Doping Control Supervisors appointed by the Sports Science and Committee;

4.2.2.2.6 up to 2 ITTF Committee or Commission Chairs nominated by the Executive Committee;

4.2.2.2.7 International Umpires, Referees and Evaluators from other Associations invited in accordance with the ITTF directives for match officials at World Title Competitions;

4.2.2.2.8 up to 7 members of the ITTF staff.

4.2.2.3 Organisers shall provide free medical care and medicine for all participants, but each Association is recommended to insure its players and officials against illness and injury for the duration of the Championships.

4.2.2.4 Organisers shall meet the cost of transport between the place of accommodation and the playing hall.

4.2.2.5 Organisers shall request their national authorities to waive visa charges for all participants.

4.2.2.6 Organisers shall ensure free access to the playing hall and free circulation therein for all the players, officials and members listed in 4.2.2.2, for any additional players and ITTF officials and for any interpreter, doctor or medical adviser appointed by the ITTF.

4.2.2.7 Organisers shall provide the ITTF with offices at the venue of the Championships and place at its disposal translation, computer, internet, telephone, telefax and duplicating facilities.

4.2.2.8 Organisers shall publish a prospectus giving the main details of the organisation of the Championships, including

4.2.2.8.1 the dates and place of the Championships;

4.2.2.8.2 the events to be held;

4.2.2.8.3 the equipment to be used;

4.2.2.8.4	the procedure for entry, the entry fees and the undertakings required;
4.2.2.8.5	the date and place of the draw;
4.2.2.8.6	the dates of Jury meetings;
4.2.2.8.7	the extent of hospitality for players and officials;
4.2.2.8.8	any directives authorised by the Board of Directors for the Championships.
4.2.2.9	During the Championships Organisers shall make available promptly to members of the ITTF Executive Committee, Board of Directors members and team captains details of results, including points scores; as soon as possible after the completion of the Championships Organisers shall publish the complete results, including points scores, and circulate them to all Associations.

4.2.3 Eligibility

4.2.3.1	Only an Association which is not in arrears (1.7.3.3) shall be eligible to enter teams or individual players in the Championships.
4.2.3.2	The system of qualification for team and individual events shall be determined by the Board not later than 18 months before the start of the Championships.
4.2.3.3	All players shall be under 19 and under 15 according to 3.7.4.2.
4.2.3.4	In addition to provisions of 3.8, players who have acquired a new nationality and wish to represent the Association corresponding to the new nationality shall register with ITTF through this new Association. A player is considered as registered either from the date of ITTF player registration confirmation or from the date the player is granted his or her new nationality, whichever is earlier.
4.2.3.5	Such player shall not represent the new Association before 3 years after the date of registration, if the player is under the age of 15 when registered, but only 1 year after the date of registration if the player has never represented another association.
4.2.3.6	Players being 15 years of age or older at the date of registration cannot represent their new Association at World Youth

Championships except that a player having participated already in World Junior/Youth Championships shall retain his or her eligibility.

4.2.4 Entry Fees

4.2.4.1 The entry fees shall be US$50 for each entry in a team event, US$30 for each pair in a doubles event and US$15 for each entry in a singles event.

4.2.4.2 The entry fees shall be paid to the organisers at the time of entry and shall be shared equally between the organisers and the ITTF.

4.2.4.3 Fees for entries from an Association are due from that Association and shall always be payable, except that the Board of Directors may waive the fees where an Association is prevented from participating in the Championships by circumstances outside its control.

4.2.5 Qualification and Entries

4.2.5.1 The intention of an Association qualified to enter teams or players shall be notified to the organisers and the ITTF in a preliminary notification form provided by the Secretariat; the closing date for the receipt of this form shall be not later than 4 calendar months before the start of the Championships.

4.2.5.2 Information shall be distributed, together with the prospectus, by the Competition Department and entries shall be submitted as required.

4.2.5.3 Two sets of these entry forms shall be returned to the organisers and one set to the Secretariat; the closing date for the receipt of these forms shall be not later than 2 calendar months before the start of the Championships.

4.2.5.4 An Association shall rank its nominated players and pairs in order of playing strength, which shall be consistent with their current ranking in the World Junior Ranking List.

4.2.5.5 Organisers may accept only formal nominations by an eligible Association, which are received, properly signed by a responsible representative of the nominating Association, on or before the closing date.

4.2.6 Modification of Entries

4.2.6.1 The nominating Association may change the composition of a team by notifying the organisers up to the time of the Jury meeting preceding the Championships, but in no circumstances after the start of the event.

4.2.6.2 As soon as he or she arrives at the Championships venue, the representative of an Association requesting a change to the draw in consequence of any error or absence shall notify the referee or his or her deputy, or confirm any change already notified, on a form provided for the purpose.

4.2.6.3 A request for modification of an entry cannot be considered unless it is made or confirmed by the representative of an Association immediately on arrival, other than a request based on the subsequent absence, illness or injury of one player of a doubles pair, which shall be made as soon as the contingency arises.

4.2.6.4 All alterations that are authorised shall be notified immediately to team captains and, where appropriate, to Association representatives.

4.2.7 Entry Obligations

4.2.7.1 The entry form shall contain a statement, to be signed by a responsible representative of the nominating Association on behalf of all its nominated players and captains, that they understand and accept the conditions of the Championships and that they are prepared to compete against all other teams and individuals participating; no entry shall be valid unless accompanied by this declaration.

4.2.7.2 In individual events all entrants are accepted as individual competitors; they shall be bound to do their utmost to win the events for which they are entered, irrespective of whether other entrants from the same Association have been accepted to take part, and they shall not withdraw except for reasons of illness or injury.

4.2.8　Jury

4.2.8.1　The Jury shall consist of the ITTF Junior Commissioner, a representative of the ITTF Competition Department, a representative of the ITTF World Junior Program, the Championships Director (or his or her equivalent), a representative of the organising committee and the referee; the referee shall have the right to speak but not to vote.

4.2.8.2　If the ITTF Junior Commissioner is unable to attend a meeting of the Jury he or she may nominate an appointee to attend in his or her place who shall have the right to speak and to vote.

4.2.8.3　The Chair of the Jury shall be appointed by the ITTF Junior Commissioner or in his or her absence by the representative of the ITTF World Junior Program.

4.2.8.4　Any Association directly affected by a matter under consideration at a Jury meeting shall be entitled to be represented at that meeting but shall not be entitled to vote.

4.2.8.5　The Jury shall have power to decide any question of appeal within the jurisdiction of a tournament management committee.

4.2.8.6　The Jury shall meet before the start of the Championships to be informed of all draw alterations requested up to that time; any subsequent questions of draw alteration shall be decided by the ITTF Junior Commissioner, and the Jury shall meet again only when convened by the Junior Commissioner to consider appeals against its administrative decisions or decisions of the referee.

4.2.9　Events

4.2.9.1　The Championships shall include boys' team and girls' team events as well as boys' singles and doubles, girls' singles and doubles and mixed doubles events.

4.2.9.2　　The system of play and the system of qualification in the team and individual events, shall be decided by the Board of Directors, on the recommendation of the Junior Commissioner, Technical Commissioner, and the Competition Department, and shall be notified to all Associations not later than 6 calendar months before the start of the Championships.

4.2.10　Default

4.2.10.1　An Association whose team is entered in the draw but which fails to compete in the event without adequate justification may be subject to disciplinary action by the AGM.

4.2.10.2　A team may begin, continue and complete a team match only with the full complement of players specified for the event, except that the referee may, at his or her discretion, allow a team to play with one player absent or an individual match to be omitted from the sequence where he or she is satisfied that the absence is due to accident, illness, injury or other circumstances outside the control of the player or the Association concerned, including disqualification by the referee in accordance with his or her authority.

4.2.10.3　An Association whose team begins to play in the event but which fails to complete its schedule of matches shall be liable to forfeit its entitlement to hospitality for its representatives at the Championships; an appeal against forfeit may be made to the Jury, whose decision shall be final.

4.2.11　Doping Control

4.2.11.1　Doping control shall be carried out in accordance with ITTF Anti-Doping rules (Chapter 5).

4.2.12　Awards and Presentations

4.2.12.1　In both team and individual events the winners shall receive gold medals, the losing finalists silver medals and the losing semi-finalists bronze medals.

4.2.12.2　At presentation ceremonies for both team and individual events the national flags of the gold, silver and bronze medal winners shall be raised and the national anthem of the gold medal winner shall be played.

4.2.13　Commercial Rights

4.2.13.1　The ITTF exclusively owns and controls all commercial rights in and to the Championships. Such Commercial Rights to include, without limitation and in each case on a worldwide basis, all:

4.2.13.1.1　audio, visual and audio-visual and data rights (in every medium, whether or not existing as at the date of these regulations);

4.2.13.1.2　sponsorship, advertising, merchandising, marketing and other forms of rights of association;

4.2.13.1.3　ticketing, hospitality and other concession rights; and

4.2.13.1.4　other rights to commercialise the Championships (including without limitation any so-called "event rights" and any right to authorise the taking of bets on the Championships.

4.2.13.2　The ITTF shall be entitled to exploit the Commercial Rights in such manner as it considers appropriate, including granting licences in respect of the same (or part thereof) to the relevant Association or to other third party(ies) from time to time.

4.2.13.3　Each Association shall ensure that their members (officials, players, delegates and other affiliates) shall:

4.2.13.3.1　comply with any and all rules, regulations and/or guidelines in relation to the exploitation of the Commercial Rights which may be issued from time to time by or on behalf of the ITTF; and

4.2.13.3.2　provide such rights, facilities and services as are required to enable the ITTF and/or the relevant third party to fulfil their obligations under any arrangements for the exploitation of any of the Commercial Rights and shall not by any act or omission infringe any exclusive rights granted there under or otherwise cause any breach thereof to occur. For the avoidance of doubt only the ITTF may enforce this rule against an Association and no third party shall be entitled to do so.

4.3 WORLD CUP

4.3.1 Composition

4.3.1.1 A World Cup for Men and a World Cup for Women shall be held on an annual basis or every 2 years in even numbered years and Continental World Cups or an equivalent shall serve as the qualification for the World Cups. The qualification and playing system will be an integral part of the ITTF's Competition Program.

4.3.1.2 Participants will be provided with free meals and accommodation from dinner on the evening before the start of the competition to breakfast on the morning after it ends; continental representatives will also be provided with free return travel tickets to the venue.

4.3.2 Authority

4.3.2.1 The ITTF shall be the sole owner of the World Cup title and tournaments.

4.3.2.2 An Association may be granted permission to organise the tournament; submission of an application to do so shall be regarded as implying knowledge and acceptance of these and all other applicable regulations.

4.3.2.3 Organisers shall not, without prior consent of the ITTF, delegate any of their authority nor make any contract or agreement with any other body, such as a Regional Association, a municipal authority or a sponsor.

4.3.2.4 Any agreement made between the organisers and any other body shall not conflict with nor derogate from the principle of these regulations; in case of any dispute the authority of the ITTF, as exercised through its representatives, shall be paramount.

4.3.2.5 The ITTF may enter into contracts with promoters or sponsors.

4.3.3   Appointments

4.3.3.1   For each tournament the ITTF Competition Department shall appoint a Tournament Director and a Competition Manager.

4.3.3.2   The Tournament Director shall be responsible to the ITTF Competition Department for ensuring observance of the conditions laid down for the tournament, including approval of the arrangements made by the organisers for ceremonies and presentations, protocol and seating arrangements at ceremonies and social functions and the presentation of play.

4.3.3.3   The Competition Manager shall be responsible to the ITTF for ensuring the adequacy of equipment and playing conditions, supervising the draw and scheduling matches.

4.3.4   Doping Control

4.3.4.1   Doping control shall be carried out in accordance with ITTF Anti-Doping rules (Chapter 5).

4.3.5   Playing System

4.3.5.1   The playing system will be determined by the Executive Committee on recommendation by the Competition Department. The selected players and their associations will be informed of the playing system to be used in the prospectus at the same time as the issuance of the invitation to the participants.

4.3.6   Eligibility

4.3.6.1   In addition to provisions of 3.8, players who have acquired a new nationality and wish to represent the association corresponding to the new nationality shall register with ITTF through this new Association. A player is considered as registered either from the date of ITTF player registration confirmation or from the date the player is granted his or her new nationality, whichever is earlier.

4.3.6.2   Such player shall not represent the new Association before:

4.3.6.2.1   3 years after the date of registration, if the player is under the age of 15 when registered, but only 1 year after the date of registration if the player has never represented another association;

4.3.6.2.2   5 years after the date of registration, if the player is under the age of 18 but at least 15 years of age when registered;

4.3.6.2.3   7 years after the date of registration, if the player is under the age of 21 but at least 18 years of age when registered.

4.3.6.2.4   9 years after the date of registration, if the player is at least 21 years old when registered.

4.3.6.3   A player having participated already in the World Cup shall retain his or her eligibility.

4.3.7   Jury

4.3.7.1   The Jury shall consist of the ITTF Executive Vice-President responsible for the World Cup, the ITTF Director of Competition, a representative of the organising committee and the referee; the referee shall have the right to speak but not to vote.

4.3.7.2   If either the ITTF Executive Vice-President responsible for the World Cup or the ITTF Director of Competition is unable to attend a meeting of the Jury he or she may nominate an appointee to attend in his or her place who shall have the right to speak and to vote.

4.3.7.3   The Chair of the Jury shall be appointed by the ITTF Executive Vice-President responsible for the World Cup.

4.3.7.4   Any Association directly affected by a matter under consideration at a Jury meeting shall be entitled to be represented at that meeting but shall not be entitled to vote.

4.3.7.5   The Jury shall have power to decide any question of appeal within the jurisdiction of a tournament management committee.

4.3.7.6   The Jury shall meet before the start of the tournament to be informed of all draw alterations requested up to that time and the Jury shall meet again only when it has to consider appeals against its administrative decisions or decisions of the referee.

4.3.8   Commercial Rights

4.3.8.1   The ITTF exclusively owns and controls all commercial rights in and to the Championships. Such Commercial Rights to include, without limitation and in each case on a worldwide basis, all:

4.3.8.1.1   audio, visual and audio-visual and data rights (in every medium, whether or not existing as at the date of these regulations);

4.3.8.1.2   sponsorship, advertising, merchandising, marketing and other forms of rights of association;

4.3.8.1.3   ticketing, hospitality and other concession rights; and

4.3.8.1.4   other rights to commercialise the Championships (including without limitation any so-called "event rights" and any right to authorise the taking of bets on the Championships.

4.3.8.2   The ITTF shall be entitled to exploit the Commercial Rights in such manner as it considers appropriate, including granting licences in respect of the same (or part thereof) to the relevant Association or to other third party(ies) from time to time.

4.3.8.3   Each Association shall ensure that their members (officials, players, delegates and other affiliates) shall:

4.3.8.3.1   comply with any and all rules, regulations and/or guidelines in relation to the exploitation of the Commercial Rights which may be issued from time to time by or on behalf of the ITTF; and

4.3.8.3.2   provide such rights, facilities and services as are required to enable the ITTF and/or the relevant third party to fulfil their obligations under any arrangements for the exploitation of any of the Commercial Rights and shall not by any act or omission infringe any exclusive rights granted there under or otherwise cause any breach thereof to occur. For the avoidance of doubt only the ITTF may enforce this rule against an Association and no third party shall be entitled to do so.

4.4 WORLD TEAM CUP

4.4.1 Composition

4.4.1.1　A World Team Cup shall be staged every 2 years in odd numbered years and the Continental Team Champions shall be invited to take part. The qualification and playing systems will be an integral part of the ITTF's Competition Program.

4.4.1.2　If the team of the host Association is qualified by its ranking at the preceding World Team Championships, then the team placing 8th at these World Team Championships shall participate.

4.4.1.3　Participants will be provided with free meals and accommodation from dinner on the evening before the start of the competition to breakfast on the morning after it ends.

4.4.2 Authority

4.4.2.1　The ITTF shall be the sole owner of the World Team Cup title and tournament.

4.4.2.2　An Association may be granted permission to organise the tournament; submission of an application to do so shall be regarded as implying knowledge and acceptance of these and all other applicable regulations.

4.4.2.3　Organisers shall not, without prior consent of the ITTF, delegate any of their authority nor make any contract or agreement with any other body, such as a Regional Association, a municipal authority or a sponsor.

4.4.2.4　Any agreement made between the organisers and any other body shall not conflict with nor derogate from the principle of these regulations; in case of any dispute the authority of the ITTF, as exercised through its representatives, shall be paramount.

4.4.2.5　The ITTF may enter into contracts with promoters or sponsors.

4.4.3 Appointments

4.4.3.1　For each tournament the ITTF Competition Department shall appoint a Tournament Director and a Competition Manager.

4.4.3.2　　The Tournament Director shall be responsible to the ITTF Competition Department for ensuring observance of the conditions laid down for the tournament, including approval of the arrangements made by the organisers for ceremonies and presentations, protocol and seating arrangements at ceremonies and social functions and the presentation of play.

4.4.3.3　　The Competition Manager shall be responsible to the ITTF for ensuring the adequacy of equipment and playing conditions, supervising the draw and scheduling matches.

4.4.4　Doping Control

4.4.4.1　　Doping control shall be carried out in accordance with ITTF Anti-Doping rules (Chapter 5).

4.4.5　Playing System

4.4.5.1　　The playing system shall be determined by the Executive Committee on recommendation by the Competition Program. The selected teams and their Associations shall be informed of the playing system to be used in the prospectus at the same time as the issuance of the invitation to the participants.

4.4.6　Eligibility

4.4.6.1　　In addition to provisions of 3.8, players who have acquired a new nationality and wish to represent the association corresponding to the new nationality shall register with ITTF through this new Association. A player is considered as registered either from the date of ITTF player registration confirmation or from the date the player is granted his or her new nationality, whichever is earlier.

4.4.6.2　　Such player shall not represent the new Association before

4.4.6.2.1　　3 years after the date of registration, if the player is under the age of 15 when registered, but only 1 year after the date of registration if the player has never represented another association;

4.4.6.2.2	5 years after the date of registration, if the player is under the age of 18 but at least 15 years of age when registered;
4.4.6.2.3	7 years after the date of registration, if the player is under the age of 21 but at least 18 years of age when registered.
4.4.6.2.4	9 years after the date of registration, if the player is at least 21 years old when registered.
4.4.6.3	A player having participated already in the World Team Cup shall retain his or her eligibility.

4.4.7 Jury

4.4.7.1	The Jury shall consist of the ITTF Executive Vice-President responsible for the World Team Cup, the ITTF Director of Competition, a representative of the organising committee and the referee; the referee shall have the right to speak but not to vote.
4.4.7.2	If either the ITTF Executive Vice-President responsible for the World Team Cup or the ITTF Director of Competition is unable to attend a meeting of the Jury he may nominate an appointee to attend in his place who shall have the right to speak and to vote.
4.4.7.3	The Chair of the Jury shall be appointed by the ITTF Executive Vice- President responsible for the World Team Cup.
4.4.7.4	Any Association directly affected by a matter under consideration at a Jury meeting shall be entitled to be represented at that meeting but shall not be entitled to vote.
4.4.7.5	The Jury shall have power to decide any question of appeal within the jurisdiction of a tournament management committee and to authorise team changes.
4.4.7.6	The Jury shall meet before the start of the tournament to be informed of all draw alterations requested up to that time and the Jury shall meet again only when it has to consider appeals against its administrative decisions or decisions of the referee.

4.4.8 Commercial Rights

4.4.8.1	The ITTF exclusively owns and controls all commercial rights in

and to the Championships. Such Commercial Rights to include, without limitation and in each case on a worldwide basis, all:

4.4.8.1.1　audio, visual and audio-visual and data rights (in every medium, whether or not existing as at the date of these regulations);

4.4.8.1.2　sponsorship, advertising, merchandising, marketing and other forms of rights of association;

4.4.8.1.3　ticketing, hospitality and other concession rights; and

4.4.8.1.4　other rights to commercialise the Championships (including without limitation any so-called "event rights" and any right to authorise the taking of bets on the Championships.

4.4.8.2　The ITTF shall be entitled to exploit the Commercial Rights in such manner as it considers appropriate, including granting licences in respect of the same (or part thereof) to the relevant Association or to other third party(ies) from time to time.

4.4.8.3　Each Association shall ensure that their members (officials, players, delegates and other affiliates) shall:

4.4.8.3.1　comply with any and all rules, regulations and/or guidelines in relation to the exploitation of the Commercial Rights which may be issued from time to time by or on behalf of the ITTF; and

4.4.8.3.2　provide such rights, facilities and services as are required to enable the ITTF and/or the relevant third party to fulfil their obligations under any arrangements for the exploitation of any of the Commercial Rights and shall not by any act or omission infringe any exclusive rights granted there under or otherwise cause any breach thereof to occur. For the avoidance of doubt only the ITTF may enforce this rule against an Association and no third party shall be entitled to do so.

4.5　OLYMPIC COMPETITIONS
4.5.1　Eligibility
4.5.1.1　To be eligible for participation in the Olympic Games a player,

coach or official shall comply with the Olympic Charter as well as with the ITTF rules. In particular the above-mentioned persons shall:

4.5.1.1.1   be entered by their National Olympic Committee (NOC);

4.5.1.1.2   respect the spirit of fair play and non-violence, and behave accordingly on the field of play;

4.5.1.1.3   respect and comply in all aspects with the World Anti-Doping Code;

4.5.1.1.4   not allow their person, name, picture or sports performances to be used for advertising purposes during the Olympic Games, except as permitted by the IOC Executive Board.

4.5.1.2   The entry or participation of a player in the Olympic Games shall not be conditional on any financial consideration.

4.5.1.3   Any player shall be a national of the country of the NOC which is entering him or her.

4.5.1.3.1   A player who is a national of 2 or more countries at the same time may represent either one of them, as he or she may elect.

4.5.1.3.2   After having represented one country in the Olympic Games, in continental or regional games or in world or regional championships recognised by the ITTF, a player may not represent another country unless he or she meets the conditions set forth in 4.5.1.3.3.

4.5.1.3.3   In addition to provisions of 3.8, players who have acquired a new nationality and wish to represent the NOC of the new association in the Olympic Games shall register with ITTF through this new Association. A player is considered as registered either from the date of ITTF player registration confirmation or from the date the player is granted his or her new nationality, whichever is earlier.

4.5.1.3.4   A player shall not represent the new NOC before:

4.5.1.3.4.1   3 years after the date of registration, if the player is under the age of 15 when registered, but only 1 year after the date of registration if the player has never represented another association;

4.5.1.3.4.2　5 years after the date of registration, if the player is under the age of 18 but at least 15 years of age when registered;

4.5.1.3.4.3　7 years after the date of registration, if the player is under the age of 21 but at least 18 years of age when registered.

4.5.1.3.4.4　9 years after the date of registration, if the player is at least 21 years old when registered.

4.5.1.3.5　If an associated state, province or overseas department, a country or colony acquires independence, if a country becomes incorporated within another country by reason of a change of border, or if a new NOC is recognised by the IOC, a player may continue to represent the country to which he or she belongs or belonged. However, he or she may, if he or she prefers, choose to represent his or her country or be entered in the Olympic Games by his or her new NOC if one exists. This particular choice may be made only once.

4.5.1.4　A player having participated already in the Olympic Games shall retain his or her eligibility.

4.5.1.5　All disputes relating to the determination of the country which a player may represent in the Olympic Games and in particular issue specific requirements relating to nationality, citizenship, domicile or residence of the player, including the duration of any waiting period, shall be resolved by the IOC Executive Board.

4.5.2　Events

4.5.2.1　The Olympic competition shall include at least men's singles, women's singles, men's team and women's team events.

4.5.2.2　The Team Match System in team events and the system of play in both team and individual events including any qualifying competitions shall be decided by the Board of Directors, on the recommendation of the Continental Council, and all Associations shall be notified in accordance with the schedule set by the IOC.

4.5.2.3　Players of the same Association shall be separated according to

3.6.3.1 and 3.6.3.3 only in preliminary rounds but not in further rounds.

4.5.3   Doping Control

4.5.3.1   Doping control shall be carried out in accordance with IOC rules and the World Anti-Doping Code.

4.6   PARALYMPIC COMPETITIONS

4.6.1   Eligibility

4.6.1.1   To be eligible for participation in the Paralympic Games a player, coach or official shall comply with the constitution of the International Paralympic Committee (IPC) as well as with the ITTF rules. In particular the above- mentioned persons shall:

4.6.1.1.1   be entered by their National Paralympic Committee (NPC);

4.6.1.1.2   respect the spirit of fair play and non-violence, and behave accordingly on the field of play;

4.6.1.1.3   respect and comply in all aspects with the World Anti-Doping Code;

4.6.1.1.4   not allow their person, name, picture or sports performances to be used for advertising purposes during the Paralympic Games, except as permitted by the IPC Governing Board.

4.6.1.2   The entry or participation of a player in the Paralympic Games shall not be conditional on any financial consideration.

4.6.1.3   Any player shall be a national of the country of the NPC which is entering him or her.

4.6.1.3.1   A player who is a national of 2 or more countries at the same time may represent either one of them, as he or she may elect.

4.6.1.3.2   After having represented one country in the Paralympic Games, in continental or regional games or in world or regional championships recognised by the ITTF, a player may not represent another country unless he or she meets the conditions set forth in 4.6.1.3.3.

4.6.1.3.3　In addition to provisions of 3.8, players who have acquired a new nationality and wish to represent the NPC of the new association shall register with ITTF through this new Association. A player is considered as registered either from the date of ITTF player registration confirmation or from the date the player is granted his or her new nationality, whichever is earlier.

4.6.1.3.4　A player shall not represent the new NPC before:

4.6.1.3.4.1　3 years after the date of registration, if the player is under the age of 15 when registered, but only 1 year after the date of registration if the player has never represented another association;

4.6.1.3.4.2　5 years after the date of registration, if the player is under the age of 18 but at least 15 years of age when registered;

4.6.1.3.4.3　7 years after the date of registration, if the player is under the age of 21 but at least 18 years of age when registered.

4.6.1.3.4.4　9 years after the date of registration, if the player is at least 21 years old when registered.

4.6.1.3.5　If an associated state, province or overseas department, a country or colony acquires independence, if a country becomes incorporated within another country by reason of a change of border, or if a new NPC is recognised by the IPC, a player may continue to represent the country to which he or she belongs or belonged. However, he or she may, if he or she prefers, choose to represent his or her country or be entered in the Paralympic Games by his or her new NPC if one exists. This particular choice may be made only once.

4.6.1.4　A player having participated already in the Paralympic Games shall retain his or her eligibility.

4.6.1.5　All disputes relating to the determination of the country which a player may represent in the Paralympic Games and in particular issue specific requirements relating to nationality, citizenship, domicile or residence of the player, including the duration of any waiting period, shall be resolved by the IPC Governing Board.

4.6.2 Events

4.6.2.1 The Paralympic competition shall include at least men's and women's class singles, men's and women's team events and any other event included by the IPC Governing Board on the recommendation of the Continental Council.

4.6.2.2 The Team Match System in team events and the system of play in both team and individual events including any qualifying competitions shall be decided by the Board of Directors, on the recommendation of the Continental Council, and all Associations shall be notified in accordance with the schedule set by the IPC.

4.6.3 Doping Control

4.6.3.1 Doping control shall be carried out in accordance with IPC rules and the World Anti-Doping Code.

4.7 WORLD PARA TABLE TENNIS CHAMPIONSHIPS

4.7.1 Authority for Organisation

4.7.1.1 The title "World Para Table Tennis Championships", referred to in this Section as "Para TT Championships", shall be bestowed by the Executive Committee on the championship events at a tournament organised by an Association entrusted with the task.

4.7.1.2 The closing date for applications to stage the Para TT Championships shall be specified by the Executive Committee and notified to all Associations, giving at least 6 months' notice.

4.7.1.3 All applications shall be considered by the Executive Committee together with the report of the Selection Committee, if applicable, on venues for the occasion in question.

4.7.1.4 Where necessary, the Executive Committee may ask one or more members of the appropriate Committee to visit the country of an Association applying for the right to organise the Para TT Championships to satisfy themselves as to the adequacy of the proposed playing and other arrangements; the cost of such visits shall be borne by that Association.

4.7.1.5　　If, after an option has been granted, circumstances change in such a way as to be likely to prejudice the satisfactory conduct of the Para TT Championships, the option may be revoked by the Executive Committee prior to the Para TT Championships.

4.7.2　Responsibilities of Organisers

4.7.2.1　　An Association granted the right to organise the Para TT Championships, hereafter referred to as the "organisers" shall be responsible for conducting them in accordance with the Laws of Table Tennis, the Regulations for International Competitions and the Regulations for World Title Competitions, as modified or supplemented by any directives authorised by the Board of Directors.

4.7.2.2　　Organisers shall provide accommodation and meals from the evening before the Para TT Championships begin until the morning after the Para TT Championships end for:

4.7.2.2.1　　members of the ITTF Executive Committee and the Para Table Tennis Committee;

4.7.2.2.2　　International Umpires and Referees from other Associations invited in accordance with directives issued by the ITTF;

4.7.2.2.3　　five international classifiers invited in accordance with directives issued by the ITTF;

4.7.2.2.4　　up to 3 members of the ITTF staff.

4.7.2.3　　If the business of the ITTF extends outside the period of the Para TT Championships the period of hospitality for those entitled to participate in such business shall be extended correspondingly.

4.7.2.4　　Organisers shall provide free medical care and medicine for all participants, but each Association must insure its players and officials against illness and injury for the duration of the Para TT Championships.

4.7.2.5　　Organisers shall meet the cost of transport between the place of arrival in the country, the accommodation and the playing hall.

4.7.2.6 Organisers shall request their national authorities to waive visa charges for all participants.

4.7.2.7 Organisers shall ensure free access to the playing hall and free circulation therein for all the players, officials and members listed in 4.7.2.2, for any additional players and committee members and for any interpreter, doctor or medical adviser appointed by the ITTF.

4.7.2.8 Organisers shall provide first-class interpreting in at least English.

4.7.2.9 Organisers shall provide the ITTF with offices at the venue of the Championships and place at its disposal translation, computer, internet, telephone, telefax and copying facilities.

4.7.2.10 Organisers shall publish a prospectus giving the main details of the organisation of the Para TT Championships, including:

4.7.2.10.1 the dates and place of the Para TT Championships;

4.7.2.10.2 the events to be held;

4.7.2.10.3 the equipment to be used;

4.7.2.10.4 the procedure for entry, the entry fees and the undertakings required;

4.7.2.10.5 the date and place of the draw;

4.7.2.10.6 the dates of Jury meetings;

4.7.2.10.7 the extent of hospitality for technical and ITTF officials;

4.7.2.10.8 accessibility for persons with a disability in the accommodation, transport and venues;

4.7.2.10.9 maximum numbers of players and officials;

4.7.2.10.10 any directives authorised by the Board of Directors for the Para TT Championships.

4.7.2.11 During the Para TT Championships Organisers shall make available promptly to members of the ITTF Executive Committee, the Para TT Committee and team managers details of results, including points scores; as soon as possible after the completion of the Para TT Championships Organisers shall publish the complete results, including points scores, and circulate them to all Associations.

4.7.3 Eligibility

4.7.3.1 Only an Association which is not in arrears (1.7.3.3) shall be eligible to enter teams or individual players for the Para TT Championships.

4.7.3.2 In addition to provisions of 3.8, players who have acquired a new nationality and wish to represent the association corresponding to the new nationality shall register with ITTF through this new Association. A player is considered as registered either from the date of ITTF player registration confirmation or from the date the player is granted his or her new nationality, whichever is earlier.

4.7.3.3 Such player shall not represent the new Association before:

4.7.3.3.1 3 years after the date of registration, if the player is under the age of 15 when registered, but only 1 year after the date of registration if the player has never represented another association;

4.7.3.3.2 5 years after the date of registration, if the player is under the age of 18 but at least 15 years of age when registered;

4.7.3.3.3 7 years after the date of registration, if the player is under the age of 21 but at least 18 years of age when registered.

4.7.3.3.4 9 years after the date of registration, if the player is at least 21 years old when registered.

4.7.3.4 A player having participated already in the World Para Table Tennis Championships shall retain his or her eligibility.

4.7.4 Entry and Capitation Fees

4.7.4.1 The entry fees shall be set by the Organisers and approved by the Para TT Committee.

4.7.4.2 The entry fees shall be paid to the Organisers at the time of entry and shall include capitation fees set by the Para TT Committee from time to time.

4.7.4.3 Fees for entries from an Association are due from that Association and shall always be payable, except that the Board of Directors may waive the fees where an Association is prevented from participating in the Para TT Championships by circumstances outside its control.

4.7.5 Submission of Entries

4.7.5.1 The closing date/s for entries shall be decided by the Organisers and approved by the Para TT Committee but shall not be later than 2 calendar months before the start of the Para TT Championships.

4.7.5.2 Entries by number and name shall be submitted on forms distributed, together with the prospectus, by the Organisers.

4.7.5.3 An Association may enter up to 3 players per class and 1 team per class per country.

4.7.5.4 An Association shall rank its players in order of playing strength, which shall be consistent with their current world ranking.

4.7.5.5 The ITTF may accept only formal nominations by an eligible Association, which are received, properly signed by a responsible representative of the nominating Association, on or before the closing date.

4.7.6 Modification of Entries

4.7.6.1 Entries by an Association may be modified with the approval of the Technical Delegate.

4.7.6.2 Entries may be modified by the referee on the advice of the Chief Classifier.

4.7.7 Entry Obligations

4.7.7.1 The entry form shall contain statements committing team members to the ITTF Anti-Doping Rules, the ITTF Classification Code, to be signed by a responsible representative of the nominating Association and all players and officials, that they understand and accept the conditions of the Para TT Championships and that they are prepared to compete against all other teams and individuals participating; no entry shall be valid unless accompanied by this declaration.

4.7.7.2　In individual events all entrants are accepted as individual competitors; they shall be bound to do their utmost to win the events for which they are entered, irrespective of whether other entrants from the same Association have been accepted to take part, and they shall not withdraw except for reasons of illness or injury.

4.7.8　Jury

4.7.8.1　The Jury shall consist of 3 representatives appointed by the Para TT Committee.

4.7.8.2　Any Association directly affected by a matter under consideration at a Jury meeting shall be entitled to be represented at that meeting but shall not be entitled to vote.

4.7.8.3　The Jury shall have power to decide any question of appeal within the jurisdiction of a tournament management committee and to authorise team and classification changes.

4.7.8.4　The Jury shall meet before the start of the Championships to be informed of all draw alterations up to that time and the Jury shall meet again to consider appeals against administrative and classification decisions or decisions of the referee.

4.7.9　Events

4.7.9.1　The Para TT Championships shall include at least men's and women's class singles, men's and women's team events and any other event included by Para TT Committee.

4.7.9.2　The system of play in events and its implementation date shall be decided by the Para TT Committee, on the recommendation of the Technical Commissioner.

4.7.10 Doping Control

4.7.10.1   Doping control shall be carried out in accordance with ITTF Anti-Doping rules (Chapter 5).

4.7.11 Awards and Presentations

4.7.11.1   In both team and individual events, the winners shall receive gold medals, the losing finalists silver medals and the winners of the bronze medal play- off bronze medals.

4.7.11.2   At presentation ceremonies for both team and individual events the national flags of the gold, silver and bronze medal winners shall be raised and the national anthem of the gold medal winner shall be played.

4.7.12 Commercial Rights

4.7.12.1   The ITTF exclusively owns and controls all commercial rights in and to the Championships. Such Commercial Rights to include, without limitation and in each case on a worldwide basis, all:

4.7.12.1.1   audio, visual and audio-visual and data rights (in every medium, whether or not existing as at the date of these regulations);

4.7.12.1.2   sponsorship, advertising, merchandising, marketing and other forms of rights of association;

4.7.12.1.3   ticketing, hospitality and other concession rights; and

4.7.12.1.4   other rights to commercialise the Championships (including without limitation any so-called "event rights" and any right to authorise the taking of bets on the Championships.

4.7.12.2   The ITTF shall be entitled to exploit the Commercial Rights in such manner as it considers appropriate, including granting licences in respect of the same (or part thereof) to the relevant Association or to other third party(ies) from time to time.

4.7.12.3   Each Association shall ensure that their members (officials, players, delegates and other affiliates) shall:

4.7.12.3.1   comply with any and all rules, regulations and/or guidelines in relation to the exploitation of the Commercial Rights which may be issued from time to time by or on behalf of the ITTF; and

4.7.12.3.2　provide such rights, facilities and services as are required to enable the ITTF and/or the relevant third party to fulfil their obligations under any arrangements for the exploitation of any of the Commercial Rights and shall not by any act or omission infringe any exclusive rights granted there under or otherwise cause any breach thereof to occur. For the avoidance of doubt only the ITTF may enforce this rule against an Association and no third party shall be entitled to do so.

4.8　WORLD VETERAN CHAMPIONSHIPS

4.8.1　Authority for Organisation

4.8.1.1　The title "World Veteran Championships", referred to in this Section as "Championships", shall be bestowed by the Board of Directors on the championship events at a tournament organised by an Association entrusted with the task.

4.8.1.2　The Championship can be organised by other bodies than Associations (area associations, clubs, etc.) if they have the necessary facilities but, an organization outside of the Association must have its sanction. The Association will be the contract partner of the ITTF.

4.8.1.3　The closing date for applications to stage Championships shall be specified by the Executive Committee and notified to all Associations, giving at least 6 months' notice.

4.8.1.4　All applications shall be considered by the Executive Committee and shall be submitted to the Board of Directors, together with the report of the Selection Committee, if applicable, on venues for the occasion in question.

4.8.1.5　Where necessary, the Board of Directors or the Executive Committee may ask one or more members of the appropriate Committee to visit the country of an Association applying for the right to organise the Championships to satisfy themselves as to the adequacy of the proposed playing and other arrangements; the cost of such visits shall be borne by that Association.

4.8.1.6 If, after an option has been granted, circumstances change in such a way as to be likely to prejudice the satisfactory conduct of the Championships, the option may be revoked by a majority vote at a Board of Directors meeting prior to the Championships; between Board of Directors meetings the Executive Committee shall have power to transfer the Championships or to take any other appropriate action.

4.8.2 Responsibilities of Organisers

4.8.2.1 An Association granted the right to organise the Championships, hereafter referred to as the "organisers" shall be responsible for conducting them in accordance with the Laws of Table Tennis, the Regulations for International Competitions and the Regulations for World Title Competitions, as modified or supplemented by any directives authorised by the Board of Directors.

4.8.2.2 Expenses for two inspection visits – usually within 6 months after the presentations and again within 6 months before the start of the event – by two (2) ITTF Competition Department members (altogether travel expenses and hospitality costs for four persons) are to be met by the organisers. Should any further visits be necessary, details will be discussed and agreed upon with the organisers.

4.8.2.3 Organisers shall provide free internal transport (between the place of accommodation and the playing venue and between the hotel and the nearest international airport upon arrival and departure) and accommodation and meals from lunch on the day before the Championships begun until breakfast on the day after the Championships end for

4.8.2.3.1 ten (10) participants (preferably 5 men and 5 women) nominated by the Executive Committee after consultation with the Veterans Committee and the Swaythling Club International (SCI);

4.8.2.3.2	three (3) persons (mainly the Computer Experts and the ITTF Competition Manager) starting five (5) days prior to the event for organisational purposes;
4.8.2.3.3	seven (7) persons to be nominated by the SCI Executive Committee, starting three (3) days prior to the event;
4.8.2.3.4	all members of the ITTF Executive Committee and the ITTF Veterans Committee Chair;
4.8.2.3.5	International umpires and referees from other Associations invited in accordance with the ITTF Directives for Match Officials at World Title Competitions; and
4.8.2.3.6	up to four (4) members of the ITTF staff.
4.8.2.4	If the business of the ITTF extends outside the period of the Championships the period of hospitality for those entitled to participate in such business shall be extended correspondingly.
4.8.2.5	Organisers shall provide free first aid/medical duty at the playing venue for all participants. All the participants are responsible for their physical and mental fitness and they must have their own health insurance against illness, accidents and injuries for the duration of the Championships.
4.8.2.6	Organisers shall provide the ITTF and the SCI with offices at the venue of the Championships and place at their disposal translation, computers, internet access, telephone and duplicating facilities
4.8.2.7	Organisers shall publish a prospectus giving the main details of the organisation of the Championships, including
4.8.2.7.1	the dates and place of the Championships;
4.8.2.7.2	the categories and events to be held;
4.8.2.7.3	the equipment to be used;
4.8.2.7.4	the procedure for entry, the entry fees and the undertakings required;
4.8.2.7.5	the date and place of the draw;

4.8.2.7.6   the dates of Jury meetings and social activities;

4.8.2.7.7   the extent of hospitality for technical officials; and

4.8.2.7.8   any directives authorised by the Board of Directors for the Championships.

4.8.2.8   During the Championships organisers shall make available promptly and regular public display of all results, including point scores.

4.8.2.8.1   Immediately after the Championships, the organisers shall present the final standings of the medallists in all age categories to the ITTF, together with photos of all medal awards to the players during the winners' ceremony.

4.8.2.8.2   All results shall be published on the official website for the event and on the ITTF official website.

4.8.3   Eligibility

4.8.3.1   All individuals who are older than 40 years of age or who will be 40 years of age in the year of the Championships are eligible to participate.

4.8.3.2   Each competitor is allowed to participate in one singles and one doubles event. In the doubles, not necessarily in one's own age category but always in the category of the younger player in the partnership.

4.8.4   Entry Fees

4.8.4.1   The entry fee and the accompanying persons fee shall be decided by the ITTF Executive Committee in conjunction with the selected Organiser.

4.8.4.2   No entry fee will be requested to the 10 invited participants listed in 4.8.2.3.1.

4.8.4.3   The entry fees shall be paid to the Organisers at the time of the entry.

4.8.5 Qualification

4.8.5.1　The Championships will be held in two stages: the qualifying competition and the competition proper. An optional consolation event will be held for players not qualified for the competition proper.

4.8.5.2　The qualifying competition will be played on the first days of the Championships, in groups. The first and second placed in each group will qualify for the competition proper. The others will have the option to play the consolation event.

4.8.5.3　If fewer than 6 players or pairs are entered in one age category the Competition Manager may decide to play a "round robin" in only one group. The exact system will be published before the start of the competition.

4.8.5.4　The competition proper and the consolation event will be played according to the knock-out system.

4.8.6 Entry Obligations

4.8.6.1　The on-line entry form shall contain statements committing the participants to the ITTF Anti-Doping Rules, requesting the acceptance of the ITTF Racket Control Regulations and confirming their availability to compete against all other individuals participating at the Championships.

4.8.6.2　All entrants are accepted as individual competitors; they shall be bound to do their utmost to win the events for which they are entered, irrespective of whether other entrants from the same Association have been entered, and they shall not withdraw except for reasons of illness or injury.

4.8.6.3　By entering the event, players agree to abide by all ITTF rules and regulations. All entered individual players agree to be under the auspices of the ITTF and its agents in all matters concerning television coverage, video, internet web casting, motion picture coverage, and photographic coverage of any kind. Participants release all rights, or rights held by their agents or sponsors, in all

171

matters relating to television and web casting coverage,video and motion picture coverage, and photographic coverage of any kind. A participant's refusal of above listed coverage may be subject to suspension or dismissal from the competition.

4.8.7 Jury

4.8.7.1 The Jury shall consist of 3 representatives: the chair of the ITTF Veterans Committee, as chair of the Jury, a representative of the Organising Committee and a representative of the ITTF Competition Department.

4.8.7.2 The referee or his/her deputy will be invited to attend the Jury meetings with the right to speak but not to vote.

4.8.7.3 The Jury shall have the power to decide any question of appeal within the jurisdiction of a tournament management committee.

4.8.7.4 Appeals can be lodged against the decision of the referees only and they have to be submitted in writing immediately after the completion of the match.

4.8.7.5 No member of the Jury can take part in the tournament as a player.

4.8.8 Events

4.8.8.1 The Championships shall include at least men's and women's singles and men's and women's doubles events.

4.8.8.2 Each event shall have the following categories of age:
40 to 44 years (+40),
45 to 49 years (+45),
50 to 54 years (+50),
55 to 59 years (+55),
60 to 64 years (+60),
65 to 69 years (+65),
70 to 74 years (+70),
75 to 79 years (+75),

80 to 84 years (+80),

85 to 89 years (+85)90 and over (+90).

4.8.8.3   If fewer than four players enter any one event, the Competition Manager has the right to either cancel the event or introduce a reasonable alternative for all concerned. Players have to be informed regarding any alterations/cancellations as soon as possible.

4.8.9   Default

4.8.9.1   Each participant is obliged to compete at the table and time set by the competition schedule.

4.8.9.2   Each participant is responsible for keeping her/himself informed when and where to play.

4.8.10   Doping Control

4.8.10.1   Doping control shall be carried out in accordance with ITTF Anti-Doping rules (Chapter 5).

4.8.11   Awards and Presentations

4.8.11.1   In all the events the winners shall receive gold medals, the losing finalists silver medals and the losers of the semi-finals bronze medals.

4.8.11.2   If there is only one group in the qualifying competition of an age category and no matches scheduled for the competition proper, medals will be presented to the 1st, 2nd and 3rd placed players/pairs of the respective group, according to the final standing of the group.

4.8.11.3   Winners and runners-up of the consolation event shall receive a small souvenir and a certificate with their names inscribed thereon.

4.8.12   Commercial Rights

4.8.12.1   The ITTF exclusively owns and controls all commercial rights in and to the Championships. Such commercial rights to include, without limitation and in each case on a worldwide basis, all:

4.8.12.1.1   audio, visual and audio-visual and data rights (in every medium, whether or not existing as at the date of these regulations);

4.8.12.1.2   sponsorship, advertising, merchandising, marketing and other forms of rights of association;

4.8.12.1.3   ticketing, hospitality and other concession rights; and

4.8.12.1.4   other rights to commercialise the Championships including without limitation any so-called "event rights" and any right to authorise the taking of bets on the Championships.

4.8.12.2   The ITTF shall be entitled to exploit the commercial rights in such manner as it considers appropriate, including granting licences in respect of the same (or part thereof) to the relevant Association or to other third parties from time to time.

4.8.12.3   All the participants at the Championships (officials, players, delegates and other affiliates) shall:

4.8.12.3.1   comply with any and all rules, regulations and/or guidelines in relation to the exploitation of the commercial rights which may be issued from time to time by or on behalf of the ITTF; and

4.8.12.3.2   provide such rights, facilities and services as are required to enable the ITTF and/or the relevant third party to fulfil their obligations under any arrangements for the exploitation of any of the commercial rights and shall not by any act or omission infringe any exclusive rights granted there under or otherwise cause any breach thereof to occur. For the avoidance of doubt only the ITTF may enforce this rule against a participant and no third party shall be entitled to do so.

4.8.13 Transitory provision

4.8.13.1   The Executive Committee shall approve the 2022 Event Guidelines in order to preserve the rights and duties for the Organisers of the 2022 World Veteran Championships according to the existing SCI rights and duties.

Index

X

Y

Z